End Times:
"Are We There Yet?"

"Dear children,
this is the last hour;
and as you have heard
that the antichrist is coming,
even now many antichrists have come.
This is how we know
it is the last hour."
1 John 2:18 NIV

End Times: "Are We There Yet?"

How Christians Are Being Steered Off Course by Misdirected Prophecy

Dr. Donald D. Hobson

Copyright 2022 by Self-Publishing School

All rights reserved. Written permission must be secured from the publisher to use or reproduce any part of this book, except for brief quotations in critical reviews or articles.

Published by Self-Publishing School, Greenville, SC

Back cover photo by Dennis Freeman, Flushing, MI

Printed in the United States of America
Painting of *Golgotha* by Ken Hobson Illustrator, Greensboro, NC
Back cover photo by Dennis Freeman, Flushing, MI
ISBN ebook: 978-0-578-29182-6
ISBN paperback: 978-0-578-29181-9
ISBN hardcover: 979-8-88759-231-2

Dedicated to my grandsons Sawyer, Luke, and John, and the grandchild on the way, that they may keep the faith of the fathers.

If you would like to receive the free *Hobson's Choice Newsletter* and get exclusive access to future books, interviews, etc., then please go to donh.authorchannel.com to join our growing community of like-minded truth seekers and Bible enthusiasts.

I covet your input as to what venues you would prefer (FB Group, blog, webinars, etc.) so that together we can touch more lives and meet people's needs.

CONTENTS

Acknowledgements viii

Foreword x

Introduction... 12

Chapter 1: The "Continental Divide" in Prophecy 19

Chapter 2: The Origins 27

Chapter 3: Steering Off Course 37

Chapter 4: Antichrist vs. Jesus Christ.. 50

Chapter 5: Pin the Tail on the Antichrist 56

Chapter 6: The Flight of the Speculative Spaceship.................. 71

Chapter 7: The Abomination of Desolation 82

Chapter 8: Jesus Was Not Wrong—or Lying!............................ 92

Chapter 9: Pictures of Jesus in the Old Testament 98

Chapter 10: Of Shepherds, Vines, and Olive Trees 111

Chapter 11: Circumcision of the Heart.................................... 118

Chapter 12: Prophecy Is Not "Rocket Science" 124

Conclusion... 128

Appendix A: Fulfillment of Daniel 9:24's Checklist of Events 133

Appendix B: Proof that Barney the Dinosaur Is the Antichrist 140

Bibliography 142

About the Author 148

ACKNOWLEDGEMENTS

Family

My wife, Tracie, for tolerating my countless hours spent in the study and for supplying the title. You are the love of my life. Where would I be without you?

Michael and Katie for their long-distance inspiration, suggestions, and support (and for our soon- to-be third grandson!).

Stephen and Kelsey, Sawyer, and Luke—thanks for the cool writer's hat to motivate me.

Laura and Garrett, and the rest of the band Phabies for inspiring me musically when I was stuck.

Rebecca and John, for your suggestions and for giving us a place to "crash" when visiting GR.

Sarah for dragging me out of my study to play games and for being your special, sweet self.

My mother, Hope, still going strong at 96, and my late father, Ken, for setting an incredible example of living a Christ-like life. I pray I can leave half that legacy behind for my children.

Friends

Special thanks to Craig Vargo and Jeff Funck for reading through my early manuscript efforts and providing insightful advice. Your wisdom was more helpful than you know.

Malcolm Smith of Malcolm Smith Ministries for instilling in me a desire to go deeper in God's Word. Your illustrations and word pictures left an impression on me since my first exposure to your teaching at a Niagara Falls conference in Buffalo, NY in 1981. Thank you does not say enough. Echoes of your teaching are sprinkled throughout this endeavor.

Sky Nuttall for your professionalism and expertise in the editing process.

Doug Ghering Art for your help with early concept sketches for potential book cover.

Cutting Edge Studios for your formatting and cover art expertise.

Kerk Murray for coaching me through the steps of publishing my first book. You are amazing!

Paula Snyder for telling me after our last high school reunion, "Just get off your butt and get it done!" You were much too nice to put it that way, but your encouraging words motivated me.

Thank you.

FOREWORD

This is a vital book that all believers should read and re-read to fully digest the truths it contains. We are living in a day when believers, especially western believers are faced with a quagmire that religion has placed in their path. The barriers blind and confuse the understanding, making the Gospel of life in Christ described in the New Testament almost impossible to lay hold of.

At the heart of the confusion is reducing the Incarnation, the Cross, and the Resurrection of Jesus as a footnote to history—especially the unfolding history of the purpose of God set forth in the Scripture. The Incarnation and the shedding of the blood of Christ stand at the center of history, the manifesting of God's eternal purpose hidden from before creation. The Christ event is the beginning of the revelation of love's purpose and simultaneously the end of all the preparation that has gone before.

All that went before is contained in prophecy and promise. These prophecies of the Incarnation and the New Covenant in the blood of Christ have been relegated by many to the end of time. Magnificent prophecies have been interpreted as a Disneyland of the future—fantasies in the same genre as Harry Potter. They become a museum of dead items for another day when they should be opening to us the Resurrection and Ascension of Jesus and made real and fresh in our lives today in the Holy Spirit.

Placing these promises at the end instead of at the beginning, while dismissing the Incarnation and work of Christ on the cross and resurrection as a failure awaiting a second chance at the end of time in a second coming, have left millions of believers students of a man-made idea.

Thank you, Don, for your research, prayer and courage in writing this book. I believe it will rescue multitudes from this blindness that has descended on the church in the last 200 years.

Your book will help lift readers out of the pit to realize Christ is All in All, the Beginning and the End, the First and the Last.

Malcolm Smith
Unconditional Love Ministries
Bandera, TX

INTRODUCTION

"We are living in the last days before Christ's Second Coming!" "He could return at any time!" These are the refrains that have pierced the ears of millions of unquestioning church-goers for centuries. The intensity was ratcheted up significantly after Israel declared its independence on May 14, 1948. End times "fever" exploded to pandemic levels with the onset of the Six-Day War in 1967. Since the early 1970s, hundreds, if not thousands, of new "prophecy gurus" have sprung up like weeds, choking out competitors in the landscape of prophetic interpretation, each extolling the virtues of their revolutionary inside knowledge of events portending the soon-coming demise of our space-time universe. The headlines have changed over the centuries, but the message has remained consistent—we are living in the final generation before Christ's Return.

With all the conflicting information swirling around in the expanding universe of prophetic interpretation, it is no wonder so many Christians come away dazed and confused. Think back to when you were first introduced to prophecy. If you had not read through the Bible previously, and you had no reason to doubt the messenger, you simply believed what you were taught. But if you *had* previously read through the Bible, especially some of the apocalyptic literature contained in it, you likely came away more confused than ever. That was my experience. I had read through the entire Bible a couple of times by the age of twelve, thanks to the encouragement (and incentives) of two very special Sunday School teachers. In high school, new teachers had full-scale religious movies at their disposal, all predicting, "The end is near." Such movies became a regular item on the teaching menu, almost as prevalent as bad food at the cafeteria. These Sunday School teachers were all sincere, godly people, but they had all learned about prophecy in the same way—from their own well-meaning Sunday School teacher, an End-Times religious movie, or a prophecy teacher (or twenty!) on television. They, too, were only teaching what they had been taught.

Bible teachers since the early 1900s have typically only been introduced to *one* interpretation. While that interpretation is fascinating, some of its core tenets are of fairly recent origin. You might be shocked to learn that the preachers advocating these new ideas were stripped of their congregations for what was considered heresy. This book inspects the foundation of the Futurist method of biblical interpretation, how that method became so wildly popular, and why we should not simply accept its claims as "Gospel." As we excavate the foundation of this view under the bright light of Scripture, you will discover that it is constructed with faulty material—material that will not pass inspection. It will be revealed that footnotes, not inspired biblical texts, compose the foundation propping up today's popular End-Times obsession. Christian believers must know that their faith rests upon the bedrock of time-tested orthodoxy, not shaky ground.

Unfortunately, Christian obsession with "Pin the Tail on the Antichrist," and an unrelenting desire to set dates for the Second Coming of Christ, has severely damaged the Church's credibility and greatly undermined the faith of thousands of Believers. We must discontinue the practice of cherry-picking only the verses that fit our desired outcome, and instead, build solely on the entire Word of God. We cannot repeat the mistake that Israel made, two millennia ago, and miss Jesus.

Israel lost her moral footing in the Old Testament and, as a result, went into exile. Worse, in the first century, many in Israel rejected Jesus as the Messiah, and within one generation, Jerusalem's literal footings were destroyed—"not one stone left

Introduction

upon another" (Matthew 24:2). Prophesy after prophesy directed the people of Israel to eagerly watch for his coming, but, taking the lead of their religious leaders, most dismissed Jesus as just another wanna-be messiah. I say most, because thousands did believe in Jesus. They heeded Jesus' warning and fled Jerusalem when they witnessed the forces of impending judgment gathering in full strength around the city.[1] Sadly, in A.D. 70, those who stubbornly rejected their Messiah had to suffer through the stench of rotting corpses and flowing blood, with neighbors eyeing their children as a possible food source.

But judgment is never God's final word; He longs for Israel to turn to Him once again. That starts with Jews coming to the realization that Jesus Christ is their Messiah. How do they do this? They need look no further than the Old Testament, for events of the first century revealed how nearly every word picture (tree, water, rock, shepherd, temple, Suffering Servant, vine or branch) pointed directly to fulfillment in the historical Jesus. Each of these "pictures of Christ" will be presented as evidence for my conclusion.

Our focus when it comes to End-Times matters should not be about proving who is right and who is wrong. Rather, our focus should be on how to reach the Jews with the knowledge that Jesus is their Messiah. Foremost, we Gentiles should thank the Jews for preserving the Scriptures, for without the Scriptures, where would we be? The Catholic Church maintained the integrity of the Scriptures, but they were not accessible to the average person. While the Reformation made the Bible available to the masses, let us not forget, if it were not for Catholic monks preserving the biblical texts, we Protestants would not even have the Scriptures!

A majority of Protestants identified the Papacy as the coming Antichrist during the Reformation, widening the schism. One doesn't have to look hard to find corruption at the head leadership of

---

[1] Luke 21:20

the Protestant or Catholic Churches. A Second Reformation is needed in our generation, one which reunites Protestants and Catholics. Let us discover ways to allow prophecy to unite rather than divide Believers. There have been enough wrong predictions concerning the identity of Antichrist and date-setting for the Second Coming that perhaps it is time to evaluate our "measuring stick." Enough of the "circular firing squads" and fierce dogmatism that plagues much of Christianity. Many gifted, orthodox Bible teachers may hold a different interpretation of a prophetic text than you but will agree with you on all the *essential* doctrines of the faith. Such diversity of opinion on interpretations can actually help strengthen the unity of the Church. Unlike merely exchanging hundred dollar bills (which leaves us exactly where we started), exchanging different ideas can be priceless. We both win. Rather than pointing fingers, let us unite over the age-old premise— "Jesus is Lord."

I respect those who hold the Scriptures in high enough esteem to defend it against all "new–comers." We are, after all, supposed to "test the spirits, to see if they are from God" (1 John 4:1). The newcomer in End-Times study (eschatology) is not the Word of God, however. The intruder is footnotes. The inclusion of footnotes, often 180 degrees opposite of Scripture, *is* new—1830s new. These footnotes are inserted right alongside holy texts and are unwittingly taken as "gospel" by many Believers. If you find yourself thinking, "I don't remember reading *that* in the Bible," join the club. Me too. In the 1970s, it was the *Thief in the Night* trilogy; more recently, the *Left Behind* series of books, video games, and movies. Soon enough, another End-Times "guru" will come along to fill the void. There is, apparently, much profit in prophet. But there is hope. The world did not come to an end by 1988 as I, and millions of other Christians, were being taught. Recent Second-Coming prognosticators have fared no better. Another generation of youth has been led to believe that Christ would return by 2000, then 2007, and surely by 2015. Such a fascination with date-setting is not healthy. It has caused

Introduction

many people, young and old, to stop building for the future, or worse, to abandon their faith altogether. Don't give up. You are not alone. Let's "connect the dots" of biblical images and symbols together so that we can walk away feeling that, even if we do not agree on every detail, there is a sense of unity and a better understanding of prophetic text**s**.

No other passage in the Bible is as important to the study of the End-Times as Daniel 9:24–27, especially verses 26 and 27. Differing interpretations of these verses have led to views that are thousands of miles apart, much like snowmelt from the peak of the Continental Divide—half the water ends up in the Atlantic Ocean and half in the Pacific. But we can maintain unity in the Church if we agree that the oceans in our illustration represent Christ and His Second Coming. We both agree that a "time of trouble" is coming before Jesus' Return; one group sees that "time of trouble" as a seven-year great tribulation, and the other sees it as the time when Satan will be "set loose for a short season." Daniel 9:26–27 is important because it is the only place in Scripture that a seven-year tribulation can be *derived*. I say derived, because the text does not state anything like, "And then shall come a time of great trouble for seven years."

My job is not to convince you that one group is right and the other wrong. It is the Holy Spirit, not me, nor any other author, who is to convince you of the truth. My goals are: (1) To provide scriptural evidence of how orthodox prophetic interpretations have been altered in recent times; (2) To present biblical alternatives to what I believe are speculative guesses; and (3) To place the focus of our attention, and especially our prayers, on the promise that Jews who were "broken off" from God's metaphorical olive tree due to their unbelief in Jesus as Messiah can be grafted back on to the tree if they do not persist in that state. My prayer is that you will have your Bible open as you read this book—studying, praying, and seeking your own conclusions. For some, this information will be unfamiliar, and the temptation is to jump immediately to the easy "fix" of labeling it as misinformation. That seems to be the quick solution today for anything we disagree with. Please consider this material as simply plain, old-fashion information. Then, you can decide for yourself where to file it.

Philosopher Karl Popper stated, "I may be wrong, and you may be right, and by an effort, we may get nearer the truth."[2] Mark Twain was blunter. Twain said, "No amount of evidence will ever persuade an idiot."[3] Not everyone will accept biblical answers; not all critters tolerate light. This book is not intended to be confrontational, but it *is* intended to challenge. As fellow "idiots," let's do what the believing citizens of Berea did and approach the Word with "all readiness of mind, *searching the Scriptures daily*, whether those things were so" (Acts 17:11).

Let me share a true story. While attending the University of Michigan, I heard an incredible display by a piano virtuoso in a church service, performed by a former graduate student of music. Her skill was on full display, and, when finished, she received the well-deserved applause. Another young woman then took her seat at the piano. Everyone was thinking, "I'd hate to follow *that*!" Then she started singing, "Jesus loves me, this I know ..." People began weeping. The first girl impressed us; the second girl moved us. I don't have the voice of Billy Graham, nor the intellect of C. S. Lewis or N. T. Wright. I do not expect to impress you. I do hope to move you. I hope to move you from merely traveling in the same direction as "the herd" to discovering what poet Robert Frost referred to as "the road less traveled." In doing so, perhaps you will find, as I did, that it made all the difference. If you have grown tired of relying upon unknown, profit-seeking tele-evangelists and End-Time

---

[2] Popper K.R. *The Open Society and Its Enemies*, Volume II, The high tide of prophecy: Hegel, Marx and the Aftermath. (London: Routledge and Kegan Paul, 1945, 5th ed, 1966), 225

[3] The Greek word for "lay person" is *idiōtēs (ιδιωτης)*. That makes those of us who are not clergy, "idiots." Hmm ...

Introduction

"gurus" for your prophetic information, then join me in a journey that is sure to surprise—in a good sort of way. Perhaps then, you can look to the future with great hope and not fear. Together, let's transform the confusing "Huh?" moments of prophetic interpretation into many exciting "Aha!" moments of discovery.[4]

Dr. Donald D. Hobson
Flushing, MI
03 MAY 22

---

[4] All scriptural references are from the *New International Version* (NIV) unless otherwise noted. Occasionally, you will come across the symbol †. Those marked with that symbol indicate original ideas I believe were revealed by the Holy Spirit. If any of these ideas are found to be helpful or enlightening, credit the Holy Spirit. If you think they are a stretch, or off-base, then blame me.

CHAPTER 1:

The "Continental Divide" in Prophecy

The Introduction mentioned the great gulf that separates various interpretations of prophecy. Granted, the language of Daniel 9 is difficult. For that reason, we will start our investigation by: (1) Quoting the text of Daniel 9:24–27, (2) Providing a brief background leading up to Daniel's vision, (3) Translating the passage in the form of two simplified paraphrases that approach the text from different perspectives, and (4) Including a side-by-side comparison of the two primary interpretations. This should provide you with a much better understanding of this difficult passage before lunging forward in our study of prophecy.

Translation of Daniel 9:24–27

> v. 24 Seventy sevens' are decreed for your people and your holy city to finish transgression, to put an end to sin, to atone for wickedness, to bring in everlasting righteousness, to seal up vision and prophecy and to anoint the Most Holy.
>
> v.25 Know and understand this: From the time the word goes out to restore and rebuild Jerusalem until the Anointed One, the ruler, comes, there will be seven 'sevens,' and sixty-two 'sevens.' It will be rebuilt with streets and a trench, but in times of trouble.
>
> v.26 After the sixty-two 'sevens,' the Anointed One will be put to death and will have nothing. The people of the prince who will come will destroy the city and the sanctuary. The

end will come like a flood: War will continue until the end, and desolations have been decreed.

v.27 He will confirm a covenant with many for *one* 'seven.' In the middle of the 'seven' he will put an end to sacrifice and offering. And at the temple he will set up an abomination that causes desolation, until the end that is decreed is poured out on him.

Historical Background

Daniel 9 opens with the prophet Daniel praying to God to act on the behalf of Israel.

He has understood from reading the book of Jeremiah that Israel's exile should be over:

> This is what the Lord says: *When seventy years are completed* for Babylon, I will come to you and fulfill my good promise to bring you back to this place.[5]

As a result, Daniel 9:19 shows the prophet crying out, "Lord, listen! Lord, forgive! Lord, hear and act!" The LORD immediately dispatches the angel Gabriel to deliver an answer to his heartfelt prayer, "Daniel, I have now come to give you insight and understanding … Therefore, consider the word and understand the vision." The vision of Daniel 9:24–27 immediately follows these words. A significant element of the vision concerns a period of time commonly referred to as "The Seventy Weeks" or the "490 Years." The text states, "seventy *sevens*," but with the passage of time, the prophecy's fulfillment in literal days, weeks, or months was eliminated, hence, the 490 *years*. Whether or not these "seventy sevens" were intended to be taken as literal or symbolic, Jesus did

---

[5] Jeremiah 29:10; cf. 25:11.

arrive on the scene, just as Daniel had prophesied, and the prophecy was fulfilled in a manner that far exceeded mere mathematics.

But not all Christians have been taught this. Millions believe the highly popular End-Times interpretation called Futurism, or Dispensationalism, which divides history into topical segments called "dispensations." According to Dispensationalists, the prophets did not "see" the modern era of the Church, or the Church Age, as they call it. They also put a major emphasis on what they believe will be a 1,000-year period of blessing, with Christ reigning the world from Jerusalem. This is not found in Daniel 9, but is derived from Revelation 20. There, the term "1,000 years" is used right alongside two other highly symbolic terms: a "chain" that binds Satan and a "bottomless pit" into which Satan is thrown. There is no chain that can bind a spirit being, and there is no such thing as a bottomless pit; it is an oxymoron. Maintaining strict literalism in regards to the 1,000 years while interpreting the chain and bottomless pit figuratively leads to confusion and inconsistency. Caution is advised against gripping too tightly to any one position. Such dogmatism is unwise when there is no consensus among Believers as to the meaning of the "1,000 years," or Millennium.[6] The three common Millennial beliefs in their most basic form are:

Amillennialism:	There is no "millennium;" The "1,000 years" of Revelation 20 are symbolic of the time of Satan's being bound at first advent.
Postmillennialism:	Christ's Second Coming will happen *after* (*post-*) a proposed "1,000 years" of Christian dominion.

---

[6] From the Latin *mille*, 1,000, and *annum*, year.

Premillennialism: Christ's Second Coming will happen *before* (*pre-*) a literal, earthly reign of Christ from Jerusalem.

There is no guarantee that *any* of them is correct. For many Christians, the idea of the Rapture, prior to a seven-year Great Tribulation, followed by a Millennium (Pre-tribulation Premillennial), is the only view advanced. It was the only option taught. I don't doubt that we may be living in the latter days prior to the Second Coming of Christ; what I question is the confident assertion made by many End-Times enthusiasts that a seven-year tribulation will be the trigger signaling that End. There are other realistic alternatives, ones that don't sacrifice orthodox principles of interpretation.

The Kingdom of God

In the Futurist interpretation of the vision in Daniel 9, Jesus' rejection by the Jews resulted in his inability to fulfill much of anything. He showed up after the expected time frame (the sixty-nine weeks), but was unable to establish his kingdom, and, therefore, his kingdom had to be deferred for an indeterminate period of time. This basic tenet of Dispensational teaching leads to the anticipation of Jesus establishing an *earthly* kingdom, in Jerusalem, for 1,000 years. Rather than living as co-heirs in the kingdom of Christ (Romans 8:17), established at his first advent, such a belief leaves only the hope of a coming Warrior-King Messiah, not unlike the Jewish hope that led to his rejection by Israel's leaders in the first century!

There are serious problems in stating that Christ's kingdom did not come but was rejected: (1) It pits one against the teaching of Jesus himself—"All authority has been given me in heaven and on earth" (Matthew 28:18); (2) It makes Jesus wrong in equating his casting out of demons with the coming of his kingdom (Matthew 12:28–29); (3) It rebuilds the wall of separation between Jews and Gentiles that Jesus' blood was shed to wash away (Ephesians 2:14); (4) It allows for the insertion of a 1,000-year *earthly* kingdom into the middle of Jesus' *everlasting* kingdom; (5) It requires the insertion of a 2,000 year (and counting) "gap" into Daniel's 490 year prophecy. Why is this so important? First, because it is contrary to so many documented Scripture passages. Second, because the foundation upon which Dispensational teaching rests is equivalent to toothpicks, and the rest of the structure is at risk of collapsing. Let's start with Daniel 9:24.

In verse twenty-four of the "Seventy Weeks" prophecy, a "checklist" of six events is recorded. This "checklist" of six events is said to be "determined" (*nechtakh*), suggesting it is to be fulfilled by the "Anointed One" when the "Seventy Weeks" are complete. Here is that checklist:

(1) To finish the transgression
(2) To make an end of sin
(3) To atone for wickedness
(4) To bring in everlasting righteousness
(5) To seal up vision and prophecy
(6) To anoint the most holy

In order to not lose focus on the purpose of this book, the scriptural evidence supporting the fulfillment of this checklist during the first advent of the Lord Jesus Christ is found in *Appendix A*.

First Paraphrase of Daniel 9:24–27 from a Partial Fulfillment View

In a vision, the angel Gabriel appeared to the prophet Daniel and revealed to him that within a period of 490 years, or "seventy weeks of years," God's Anointed One, the Messiah, would come to Israel. This Messiah would fulfill a checklist of events and usher in the New

Covenant (that Jeremiah 31:31–34 had prophesied), prior to being "cut off," in the middle of the 70th week. As a result of Israel killing the Messiah, God would send armies from the ruling empire to punish Israel and to destroy all vestiges of the old covenant: the temple in Jerusalem, the priesthood, the meritocracy of the Law, even the city itself. Not one stone would be left upon another.

Second Paraphrase of Daniel 9:24–27 from a Futurist View

In a vision, the angel Gabriel appeared to the prophet Daniel and revealed to him that a period of 490 years, or "seventy weeks of years," was to come, leading up to the appearance of God's Anointed One, the Messiah, to Israel. After sixty-nine weeks of years, but before the seventieth, Israel rejected God's Anointed One. As a result of him being put to death, he was not able to fulfill the items on Gabriel's checklist, and his kingdom was not established but deferred. God's "prophetic clock" stopped at this time, and it will not start up again until God turns His attention back to Israel when the Antichrist appears and the Church is snatched away in what is called the Rapture. The Antichrist will be hailed as a great leader for bringing stability to Israel and the Middle East in the form of a seven-year peace agreement. In this new era of peace and prosperity, Temple sacrifices will be resumed as in ancient times (a new Jewish temple will have been rebuilt by this time). But after three-and-a-half years, the Antichrist will violate that peace agreement and proceed to set up an idol, perhaps a statue of himself, within the Temple. Antichrist will destroy this Temple, along with the city of Jerusalem, and wreak havoc in the most violent period in all of history. The Church will experience the Rapture before the persecution of the Antichrist takes effect (Pre-Tribulation) when

End Times: "Are We There Yet?"

Christ comes *for* his saints.[7] After the seven-year Great Tribulation, this "Lawless One" will be killed when Christ comes *with* his saints. Christ will then reign from his throne in Jerusalem for 1,000 years, as the Jews will finally recognize him as their Messiah.

The first paraphrase is shared by those who believe that Jesus was "cut off" after three- and-a-half years of ministry, the second three-and-a-half-year period being the preaching of the Gospel "to the Jew first." Jesus' sacrifice is seen as the once-for-all sacrifice for sin—the final Passover. The second paraphrase is the view held by those who believe the events in the text are yet future, hence, Futurist. Dispensationalists/Futurists are Premillennial in their belief.

General Outline of the Two Primary Interpretations of Daniel 9:24–27

Partial Fulfillment View	**Futurism's View**
Messiah is the subject	Antichrist is the subject
70 consecutive weeks ("490 Years")	69 weeks ... 2,000+-year gap ... 70th week
Messiah has 3.5-yr ministry after 69th week	Messiah rejected; 70th week deferred
Jesus confirms the New Covenant (Luke 22:20)	Antichrist will make covenant with Israel
Kingdom of God established (Mt.12:29; 28:18)	Kingdom rejected; awaits *earthly* kingdom
Messiah "cut off" in midst of 70th week	Covenant broken in midst of 7-yr agreement

---

[7] Not all Dispensationalists ascribe to a Pre-Tribulation rapture. Some believe the Rapture will occur in the midst (Mid-Trib) or after (Post-Trib) the Great Tribulation of the 70th Week.

The "Continental Divide" in Prophecy

Armies destroy Jerusalem/temple in A.D. 70	Idol to be set up in future rebuilt temple
A.D. 70 was the time of great tribulation	Great Tribulation = 70th week/Antichrist

This side-by-side comparison of the two positions is, perhaps, the most important point of the book for understanding just how the two camps have ended up "thousands of miles apart." For 1,800⁺ years, the Church was mostly united on these matters, but then it all changed.

CHAPTER 2:

The Origins

Dispensationalism and the "1,000 Years"

The "father of Dispensationalism" is John Nelson Darby.[8] Darby was an Anglo-Irish Bible teacher from London who made trips to Edinburgh, Scotland, where he first heard the unorthodox millennial teachings of Edward Irving. Irving had translated some apocalyptic writings of Jesuit Manuel Lacunza in 1827, which explored new vistas in regards to the Second Coming and the humanity of Jesus. When he began to stray from orthodox beliefs, even Irving's dearest friends abandoned him. He was excommunicated by the presbytery of London in 1832 and condemned by the General Assembly of the Church of Scotland the following year. Darby, however, intrigued by Irving's approach to interpretation, began teaching that Christ would come in the form of a secret rapture *before* a Great Tribulation, followed by an earthly 1,000-year reign of Christ. Though accepted today by most evangelicals, this teaching was considered heretical at the time because it lacked historical roots. Like Irving, Darby was stripped of his clerical position. Irving would found the Catholic Apostolic Church, and Darby splintered off from the Plymouth Brethren, forming an even more anti-establishment church called the

---

[8] For those who wish to pursue Dispensational origins further, check out: Francisco Ribera, Manuel Lacunza, Edward Irving, Margaret McDonald, Cardinal Robert Bellarmine, William E. Blackstone, and Arno Gaebelein.

The Origins

Exclusive Brethren, aka—Darbyites.[9] He introduced his novel interpretations to America around 1830.

The four basic tenets of Dispensational teaching include: (1) Dividing history into topical periods called dispensations; (2) Pre-Millennialism; (3) Pre-tribulation rapture; and (4) Zionism (All of these terms will be explained in greater detail as we move forward). Initially, Darby's ideas did not gain much traction, but they gained a major boost with the publication of William E. Blackstone's *Jesus Is Coming* in 1889. Blackstone was most famous of the Zionist millenarians, who attempted a political realization of his beliefs in the future of the Jews in the Land of Israel through memoranda to the President of the United States in 1891 and in 1916.[10] The growth of Premillennial Dispensationalism then exploded when Darby disciple, Cyrus I. Scofield, published his footnotes alongside Scripture in his *Scofield Reference Bible* in 1909. Joseph M. Canfield, author of *The Incredible Scofield and His Book*, calls into question the seriousness of Scofield's motives and scholarship, exposing the questionable background and faulty theology of the man most responsible for the popularity of the dispensational system today.[11] Personally, I think that Canfield went too far in his *ad hominem* attacks. Scofield is human, and it is my belief that he was unwittingly used by the wealthy oligarchs of his day to help promote the Zionist cause—restoring the Jews to their original homeland.[12]

---

[9] Irving's death in 1834, one year after being deprived of his status as a clergyman, was attributed to tuberculosis and a broken heart. From Ralph Woodrow. *Great Prophecies of the Bible* (Riverside, CA: Ralph Woodrow Evangelical Association, Inc., 1989), 36. *Great Prophecies of the Bible* is a good source of information on Dispensational history.

[10] *Encyclopedia Judaica*, (Jerusalem: Keter Publishing House Jerusalem Ltd., 1972), 1154. Interestingly, neither Scofield nor his *Scofield Reference Bible* are mentioned in *Encyclopedia Judaica*.

[11] Joseph M Canfield, *The Incredible Scofield and His Book,* (Valecito, CA: Ross House Books, 1988).

[12] Rothschild money helped the Jews return to Israel. Lionel Walter Rothschild was a Zionist and was the recipient in 1917 of the Balfour Declaration, in which

He was definitely influenced by Darby. The distinction they make between Israel and the Gentile nations fits perfectly with the Zionist agenda. Futurists make up a large percentage of those supporting Christian Zionism. Supporting Israel is seen by them as a form of "blessing Abraham," in accordance with the promise to Abram in Genesis 12:3, "I will bless those who bless you, and curse those who curse you." That promise goes on to say that, through Abram, "All the nations of the world will be blessed." All nations includes Israel, but dividing the world into Jew and Gentile goes against the message of the New Testament.

This merger of Dispensationalism and Zionism is reminiscent of Sarah and Abraham's scheme to "help God out" in producing the promised child. Trying to help God doesn't usually work out too well. Their compromise birthed Ishmael, of whom Scripture says,

> He will be a wild donkey of a man; his hand will be against everyone and everyone's hand against him, and he will live in hostility toward all his brothers.
> –Genesis 16:12

Most of the Middle East problems today can be traced back to this event. Money from extremely wealthy, non-Christian Jews, in conjunction with the support of Christian Zionism, certainly helped return the Jews to Palestine. Christians who are not actively supporting Israel financially are often considered Anti-Semitic. This is ironic, since the Lord Jesus Christ, whom we worship, *is* a Jew!

While Dispensational teaching sprung up fairly recently with John Darby, we need to go back in history to understand how the fascination with the "1,000 Years" took root. As far back as the first

---

Britain gave its support for the establishment of a "national home for the Jewish people" in Palestine. Samuel Untermyer, agent of Lord Rothschild, acted as the liaison between Scofield and the British Zionists at Oxford University. He may have been Scofield's sponsor for membership in the exclusive Lotus Club of New York.

The Origins

century, teachers claiming to possess special revelation or knowledge (*gnosis*) roamed about sowing the seed of an earthly 1,000-year reign of Messiah. Cerinthus was one such Gnostic teacher espousing millennial concepts. Many scholars believe that John wrote his Gospel to counter the foreign teachings of Cerinthus, an Ebionite arch-heretic.[13] Ebionites were an early Christian sect who believed Jesus was the Messiah but denied his divinity and virgin birth and insisted upon keeping the old Jewish laws and rituals.

    A popular story tells of the apostle John jumping up and warning everyone to flee a Roman bath house because the heretic Cerinthus was there, and he didn't want anyone to be killed if God decided to collapse the building in righteous judgment![14] The concept of this earthly reign centers around the "1,000 years" of Satan being bound in Revelation 20:1–7 and combining it with the idea of a final "dispensation" at the end of time and space. The popular term "Millennium" refers to this period of time, as it is derived from the Latin *mille*, "1,000," and *annum*, "years."[15] In recent decades, the "Millennium" has developed into an ideology unto itself. Over time, this 1,000-year period has become associated with Futurism's final "dispensation," which they call the Kingdom Age, or the Millennium. To be safe, I recommend sticking to the biblical term "1,000 years" and determining for yourself whether the term is meant to be taken literally or symbolically. Get nervous any time someone claims to have an intellectually superior "Christian doctrine." The greatest safeguard is the Bible itself.

    The Church needs to concern itself with prophetic matters, or it runs the risk of repeating the mistakes that Israel made in the

---

[13] David Chilton, *The Days of Vengeance: An Exposition of the Book of Revelation,* (Tyler, TX: Dominion Press, 1987), 494.

[14] This story was passed down by 1st Century bishop Polycarp to Irenaeus, as recorded in Irenaeus, *Against Heresies*, i.xxvi.1-2; iii.4

[15] *Chiliasm* is the Greek term for the "1,000 years."

Old Testament. Prophetic texts are important—both the fulfillments and the failures. Israel was supposed to be the "light to the nations" but failed miserably. The Jews had that honor stripped from them when they rejected Jesus as their Messiah. The kingdom was taken from them and granted to the Gentiles, as depicted in Jesus' Parable of the Vineyard Owner:

> Therefore, I [Jesus] say unto you, *The kingdom shall be taken from you*, and given to a nation bringing forth the fruits of it.
> –Matthew 21:33–44

The apostle Paul supports this idea. Israel was "broken off" the metaphorical olive tree, he says, due to unbelief, and he hopes they will repent and be brought back into the kingdom:

> But if their [Jews] transgression means riches for the world ... how much greater riches will their full inclusion bring ... what will their acceptance be but life from the dead? ... And *if they do not persist in unbelief, they will be grafted in*, for God is able to graft them in again ...
> –Romans 11:12–26

The fulfillment of this prophecy, the grafting of the Jews back into God's kingdom, should be near the top of every Christian's prayer list (right up there with your neighbor's seventy-year-old cousin's arthritis!). Helping the downcast was one of the proofs that Jesus was, indeed, the Messiah. Christians risk failure when they neglect to provide aid for the poor and needy—financially and spiritually. The Church does not need prophetic texts to remind them of their duty to care for the less fortunate, but they must not forget Paul's earnest prayer and prophecy for his unrepentant countrymen. Most modern Jews are spiritually "downcast." Secular concerns have supplanted those of their once-treasured Messiah. Money and Torah are the new gods; without Jesus, that is all they have left.

The Church will require the assistance of believing Jews if they are to be successful in carrying forth the message that the "lost sheep" of Israel can be grafted back into the fold, fulfilling the prophecy of Romans 11.

Division Hurts Division in the Body of Christ hurts Christianity. You may be thinking of church splits that have occurred over seemingly trivial matters—the length or quality of the pastor's sermons, the style or volume of music, the color of choir robes, etc. A more serious division, one that cuts at the very heart of Christianity, is the one that separates members of the Church based purely on genealogy. Scofield's footnote on 2 Kings 17:23 states, "Although Israel is now in age-long dispersion because of their rejection of their Messiah, nevertheless they will continue as a people, preserved *distinct from other peoples* ..." That is *not* the message of the New Testament.

The Church held a position of great esteem in every field of endeavor throughout the centuries: Science, Literature, Art, Music, Philosophy, etc. Enemies of the Faith are continually attempting to undermine the advances of Christianity, feverishly chipping away at the three foundational principles upon which all those "pillars" rest– –Knowledge, Morals, and Being.[16] Remove any one of these foundational principles and our entire worldview, Christian or otherwise, crumbles to the ground. Under the guise of glowing-sounding terms, "Enlightenment" or "Woke," they promote all that is opposed to the *Imago Dei* ("Image of God"). That is why sex and violence are Satan's chief weapons tearing at the fabric of civil

---

[16] Greg Bahnsen, *Defending the Christian Worldview Against All Opposition, Series One: Weapons of Our Spiritual Warfare*, (Powder Springs, GA: American Vision, 2006), Disc 8: *A Critique of Atheism*. The fancy term for these "foundation stones" is Epistemology, Ethics, and Metaphysics (Reality).

society. Our bodies are considered the temple of the Holy Spirit, and we represent God's image. Violence rips at that image, and sexual deviancy defiles the glorious temple that is the human body.

Christianity is intended to be the "light of the world" and the "salt of the earth." Sadly, the influence of the Church in society has been greatly diminished, if not outright dismissed, in modern Academia. She is marginalized in many circles because of: (1) Her obsession with End-Times matters that are none of our business; (2) Date-setting prophecies that are continuously proven to be false;[17] (3) Interpretations that are so far removed from the text of Scripture that confusion, rather than knowledge, reigns; and (4) The Churches' strong-held belief in prophecy and miracles grates against the Naturalistic scientific community's *a priori* dismissal of all things supernatural. Christians should not apologize for a belief in the supernatural, as nearly every Christian reading this book can attest to at least one event in his or her past that is unexplainable in natural terms. Most non-Christians believe in the spirit world, too, only their obsessions lean more to the occultic, dark side. The arguments of atheists and agnostics hold no meaning to those who have experienced spiritual supernatural events. But this fascination with all things End-Time is not healthy for the Church. How did Christians end up on "opposite sides of the mountain" when it comes to the interpretation of important prophetic texts? Let's take a look, for it starts right at the beginning—in Genesis.

Genesis One and Two Footnotes

I hate to use the word "indoctrination," but how else can you explain some of the early footnotes in the *Scofield Reference Bible*? For example, here is what Genesis 1:28 states,

---

[17] A prime example of this comes from Hal Lindsey's book *The 1980s: Countdown to Armageddon*, where he states, "The decade of the 1980s could very well be the last decade of history as we know it."

The Origins

> God blessed them and said to them, Be fruitful and increase in number; fill the earth and subdue it. Rule over the fish in the sea and the birds in the sky and over every living creature that moves on the ground.

Scofield breaks history up into seven dispensations based on this lone, non-supporting verse!

Scofield's seven dispensations:

1. Innocence
2. Conscience
3. Human Government
4. Promise
5. Law
6. Church
7. Kingdom (Millennium)

They are not in the text.

He performs similar interpretational "magic" with Genesis 2:16–17, which reads,

> And the Lord God commanded the man, "You are free to eat from any tree in the garden; but you must not eat from the tree of the knowledge of good and evil, for when you eat from it you will certainly die."

Scofield manages to discover six additional covenants to the old and new covenants that are mentioned in Scripture (his Mosaic covenant is equivalent to the old covenant, or the Law).

Scofield's eight major covenants:
1. Edenic
2. Adamic
3. Noahic
4. Abrahamic
4. Mosaic
6. Palestinian
7. Davidic
8. New Covenant

In lengthy footnotes attached to these verses, he does not refer you to scriptural texts describing, explaining, or supporting his claims. He can't. They are not there. Rather, he *directs you to more of his footnotes*![18] He does this in an attempt to garnish support for his conclusions, but Genesis 1:28 and 2:16–17 say nary a word concerning multiple dispensations or covenants. This does not stop Scofield from creating a whole new dispensation (one the prophets apparently did not see), just for us—the Church Age. Keep in mind, without his dispensational foundation, his whole interpretational structure collapses. Dispensational teaching has forever altered the landscape of prophetic interpretation. But there is hope. Careful examination of the actual texts will help us navigate through this prophetic "minefield" unscathed. If you are wondering whether or not you have been influenced by some of these questionable teachings, check out the lists above. If you recognize some of these items, then yes, somewhere along the line, you have been exposed to Dispensational "Truth." Dispensationalists refer to their teaching as "Rightly dividing the Word of God," but it often ends up dividing

---

[18] I have compiled a list of 95 footnotes in the 1967 edition of the *Scofield Reference Bible* that contradict Scripture or where he remains silent on passages that are in direct opposition to his footnotes. That book was originally intended to be published first, but since this is a first "go-around," it seemed prudent to tackle something more manageable.

The Origins

the people of God.[19] Now that we have seen how Scofield laid the foundation for Futurism in Genesis, let's see how it altered the structure of Daniel's vision.

---

[19] Clarence Larkin, *Dispensational Truth or God's Plan and Purpose in the Ages,* (Glenside, PA: Rev. Clarence Larkin Est., 1918), p.1. Larkin uses the phrase "Rightly Dividing the Word of Truth" in the Foreword of his fascinating book of charts and drawings. His Foreword also includes these interesting comments: (1) When he [Larkin] entered the Gospel Ministry direct from business and *without any previous theological training...*, and (2) he was not a premillennialist at the time of his ordination but his study of the Scriptures, *aided by some books that fell into his hands*, led him to adopt that view (italics added for emphasis). Unfortunately, Larkin does not divulge which books "fell into his hands."

CHAPTER 3:

Steering Off Course

Recall that the Seventy Weeks in Daniel's vision is equivalent to the 490 Years. The number "490," which plays such a prominent role in Daniel's vision, is no accident. Mathematically, it can be broken down in a couple of interesting ways:

$$70 \times 7 = 490$$
$$10 \times 49 = 490$$

70 x 7

Israel struggled under a burden of *physical* exile in Babylon for seventy years; her *spiritual* exile would last 70 x 7 years! Can you think of any place else where reference is made to 70 x 7? Ah, when Peter came to Jesus and asked, "Lord, how many times shall I forgive my brother or sister who sins against me? Up to seven times?" Jesus' reply is telling, "I tell you, not seven times, but *seventy times seven*."[20] Some have translated this as *seventy-seven times*, but this shatters a beautiful picture of Jesus as the "Ultimate Jubilee," the Anointed One of God. Moses made the same mistake. In disobeying God's command to "speak to the rock" to bring forth water in the wilderness, and instead, smiting the rock a second time, Moses smashed a beautiful picture of Christ *smitten once*, and only once, on the cross, setting free all who were held captive to sin.

---

[20] Matthew 18:21–22. "Seventy-seven" times is wrong here (see NIV text note). The Greek here does not support it, and, as stated above, it destroys a beautiful picture of Jesus as the "Ultimate Jubilee."

Shattering beautiful pictures of Christ keeps one out of the Promised Land—just ask Moses (Numbers 20:7–12).

Jesus seems to be saying, "Forgive them unto me." No other religion or person offers forgiveness for sin past, present, and future. Many religions offer methods of keeping on the straight and narrow path, from a point of commitment, but only Christianity can help you with *past* sin. That should be a great comfort to those struggling under a burden of guilt and shame. The name Jesus means "salvation;" he entails what forgiveness is all about. He is also what the number 490 is all about.

10 x 49

Ten is considered to be the number of *quantitative* completion.[21] It is used to express totality. Forty-nine is significant because, after every forty-nine years, Israel was to celebrate a year of Jubilee—a year of liberation, when debts were cancelled, slaves set free, and property was returned to whoever owned it (Leviticus 25). Judah's failure to acknowledge the demands of Jubilee landed them in Babylonian exile for seventy years. Her *spiritual exile* will last for seventy times seven years. Jesus is the "Ultimate Jubilee" that the Year of Jubilee pointed to, but ... there is a problem. Jesus could only be the fulfillment of the original Jubilee if he truly ushered in God's kingdom. What does Jesus have to say about this? In his post-resurrection appearance in Matthew 28:18 he states, *"All authority has been given me* in heaven and on earth."

---

[21] The number ten is considered to be the number of *quantitative* completeness, because, once you get to 10, you start over with 11, 12, etc.). The number seven is referred to as the Divine number of *qualitative* completion.

Reconstructing "The Wall"

If we accept the assertion of Scofield, that a distinction should be maintained between Jew and Greek, then what is a Christian to do with well-known scriptural passages like:

> *There is neither Jew nor Gentile*, neither slave nor free, nor is there male and female, for you are all one in Christ Jesus.
> –Galatians 3:28

> This mystery is that through the gospel the *Gentiles are heirs together with Israel*, members together of *one body*, and sharers together in the promise in Christ Jesus.
> –Ephesians 3:6

> For he himself is our peace, who has made the two groups one and has destroyed the barrier, the dividing wall of hostility
> –Ephesians 2:14

This sure sounds like the unity of Jews and Gentiles in Christ, not distinction.

Another seemingly insurmountable wall has been erected by Futurists with their installation of a 2,000 year (and counting!) "Gap" between the 69th and 70th weeks of Daniel's prophecy. This "Gap," or "Parenthesis," creates crippling problems. First, it is arbitrary and inconsistent, and that makes the argument illogical.[22] Second, it makes Daniel out to be a false prophet! The guide to determine if someone was a false prophet was whether or not their prophecy came true.

---

[22] Bahnsen, *Defending the Christian Worldview*, Disc 8.

> How can we know when a message has not been spoken by the Lord? *If what a prophet proclaims in the name of the Lord does not take place or come true,* that is a message the Lord has not spoken. That prophet has spoken presumptuously …
> –Deuteronomy 18:21–22

Daniel said, "Seventy weeks [sevens] were *determined* …" He said nothing about prophetic clocks, a gap, or any other disruption to the 70 weeks. Third, the "Gap" becomes the hammer necessary to pound the vision into a shape that will adapt to their interpretation. In actuality, the interpretation should fit the vision. This arbitrary "Gap" has done more to widen the literal gap between the two extremes of interpretation than any other thing. On one extreme, you have those who believe that the 70th week followed in logical, consecutive order immediately after the sixty-nine weeks. It refers to the coming "Anointed One," or Messiah, who would be cut off in the middle of the 70th week. At the other extreme, you have those who believe that the 70th week is still in our future and is about an individual Antichrist figure who will come and make a treaty with Israel for seven years but who will then break that treaty in the middle of the 70th week. Like I said, "Thousands of miles apart."

Consider this illustration. You are in your car heading for a major city that is seventy miles from where you live (Detroit in this case). As you enter the expressway a sign confirms what you already knew: "Detroit—70 miles." You drive most of the way there, 69 miles to be exact, when you pass a sign stating, "Detroit—2,000 miles?" At first you might be confused, thinking that some incompetent highway worker needs to lose their job. Despite being navigationally challenged, you know you didn't make *that* big of a mistake. More likely you'd be steamed. "I know my way to Detroit" you grumble to yourself. But that is the reasoning you are expected to swallow if you tow the Futurist line. Please forgive my "road rage" that flares any time I hear my fellow Christians being offered this 2,000-mile detour around Daniel's vision.

A simplified diagram of the two positions should aid in visualizing the differences (not to scale). Noting the position of the 70th Week in each diagram will be helpful, keeping in mind that 2,000 years separate them. You may also find it helpful to expand these diagrams, making it closer to scale and easier to decipher. Making the second diagram to scale will be difficult, as the "Gap" takes up nearly four times the length of Daniel's original vision.[23]

Partial Fulfillment Timeline

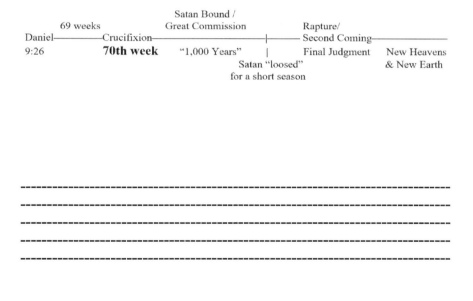

---

[23] Larkin, Clarence. *Dispensational Truth or God's Plan and Purpose in the Ages*, (Rev. Clarence Larkin Est.: Glenside, PA), chart on p. 139½. Larkin's chart depicts the toes in Daniel 2's statue as significantly lengthened, but they would need to be 3-4 times longer in his diagram to accurately portray his interpretation.

Futurist Timeline

```
                                    Pre-, Mid-,
                                    or Post-trib.
         69weeks      2,000-year    RAPTURE
Daniel———————Stop———————————————————70thWeek————Millennium————————————
9:26                  "Gap/Parenthesis"  3½ + 3½     1,000 Years    New Heavens
                                         Great Trib;  Earthly reign  & New Earth
                                         Covenant w.  in Jerusalem
                                         Israel made
                                         then broken
```

The simplicity of the Partial Fulfillment interpretation reminds me of Jesus' parables—something that the average person can easily understand. He wanted his listeners to grasp his meaning. Contrast that with the flurry of activity centered around the delayed 70th week in the Futurist position. Several other events must take place *prior to* the 70th week in order to fit their interpretation: (1) A new temple must be rebuilt at, or in very close proximity to, the Dome of the Rock, the Muslim mosque presently occupying the site; (2) the Roman Empire must be revived in some form (the European Union being the favorite choice in recent decades); (3) a new Jewish priesthood must be ordained, despite the lack of genealogical records required for the position because they were destroyed in the fires of A.D. 70; (4) re-institution of animal sacrifices must take place; (5) an individual Antichrist figure will have to arrive who will deceive Israel by means of a seven-year treaty that he will then break; (6) the institution of this treaty between Antichrist and Israel is the event that will usher in what the Futurist refers to as the Great Tribulation.

While both parties anticipate a time of terrible affliction before Christ's Second Coming, they disagree on who the Olivet Discourse was addressed to and to what period of time it should be assigned. Partial Fulfillment advocates believe Jesus was addressing this message to his first-century followers, preparing them mentally and physically for the existential threat that would soon befall them– –"before *this generation* passes" (Matthew 24:34). Christians in

Jerusalem were to expect a time of great persecution and apostasy, when even family members would turn on one another.[24] They were also to be on the lookout for armies besieging the city; when the opportunity to flee comes—seize it! Believers who hold to a first-century fulfillment of the Olivet Discourse still anticipate a time of great distress prior to Jesus' Second Coming but only after the *figurative* 1,000 years of Satan's binding is over. At that time, he is set loose (perhaps he thinks he escaped), as he is emboldened to gather all of the forces of evil in the world against the followers of Christ[25] Many wonder whether that season is upon us now.

Futurists, on the other hand, claim Jesus' message is intended for Believers living in the generation just before his Second Coming. The intense persecution will come, not by Roman armies, but by a world ruler, Antichrist, who will come to power and inflict Great Tribulation upon the Jews. Christians have nothing to fear, according to Pre-tribulationists, as they will have been snatched away in the Rapture prior to the onslaught of the Antichrist's vicious assault. They adamantly believe Christians are living in the terminal generation. So did Protestants living at the time of the Reformation––500 years ago. Periodically they need to be reminded that, until a new temple is built, none of these other "signs of the times" matter. Antichrist cannot set up his idol-image in a temple that does not exist.

Anticipation of Jesus' Return was heightened for Futurists after Israel achieved its independence on May 14, 1948. This anticipation reached a fever pitch in the 1970s-80s, with books like Hal Lindsey's *Late Great Planet Earth* and Ken Whisenut's *88 Reasons Jesus Will Return in 1988*. Second Coming Fever spiked again with the *Y2K* scare and 2015's *Four Blood Moons* watch. Such

---

[24] The Greek word *thlipsis* can be translated as affliction, tribulation, or persecution.
[25] Satan being set free for a short season is found in Revelation 20:3, 7.

headline hunting for prophetic fulfillments will continue unabated as long as a gullible population is willing to gobble it up.[26] Anyone with more than two functioning senses can see and feel that things are different now. Something is going on that we just can't put our fingers on. Conspiracy theories abound about the tentacles of the Rothschild family and their centuries-old push for control over a one-world government. The average citizen has no clue as to the veracity of these claims. We need to remind ourselves that Jesus is Lord—not Caesar, not the Rothschilds, but Jesus. During these times of discontent and uncertainty, it is imperative that we never lose sight of the Great Commission—"Therefore go and make disciples of all nations, baptizing them in the name of the Father and of the Son and of the Holy Spirit, and teaching them to obey everything I have commanded you. And surely, I am with you always, to the very end of the age." We all look forward to the most important thing, Christ's Return, so let's "be ready" when he does.

One final note in regards to the "Gap." It becomes totally unnecessary when the claim "Jesus was rejected" is removed. It is true that Jesus was rejected by some—unbelievers! But the Church in its infancy grew by means of *believing Jews.* If the claim that the Jews rejected Jesus is a "thorn in your side," these scriptural examples should help pull it out of your flesh.

> Those who accepted his message were baptized, and about *three thousand were added* to their number that day. And the Lord added to their number daily those who were being saved.
> —Acts 2:41, 47

---

[26] Such reading the "news of the day" *into* the text is called eisegesis, as opposed to exegesis, the drawing *out of* the text. A good example of that is Jonathan Cahn's *The Paradigm,* where he equates Bill and Hillary Clinton, President Obama, and President Trump to Ahab and Jezebel, Jehoram/Joram (king of Israel), and Jehu, king of Judah!

> But many who heard the message believed; so the number of men who believed grew to about *five thousand*.
> —Acts 4:4

> Nevertheless, *more and more men and women believed* in the Lord and were added to their number.
> —Acts 5:14

> When they heard this, they praised God. Then they said to Paul: You see, brother, how *many thousands of Jews have believed*, and all of them are zealous for the law.
> —Acts 21:20

Can we please put the claim "The Jews rejected Jesus" to rest once and for all? The kingdom of God was to be presented to the Jews first, the "lost sheep of Israel." It was only after the Jews began rejecting Paul and Barnabas, and opposing the Gospel of Jesus Christ, that the apostle Paul turned and said to the Jews,

> We had to speak the word of God to you first. Since *you reject it* and do not consider yourselves worthy of eternal life, *we now turn to the Gentiles*. For this is what the Lord has commanded us: I have made you a light for the Gentiles, that you may bring salvation to the ends of the earth.
> —Acts 13:46–47

Paul is quoting from Isaiah 49:6 and applying that Old Testament promise to himself. He will now go forth determined that nothing short of death will stop him from fulfilling his new role as the apostle to the Gentiles. This is not God's "plan B." God's original promise to Abram was "through you, *all the nations of the world will be blessed*" (Genesis 12:3). Abraham looked forward to the day when people would be delivered from sin and spiritual exile and ushered into "a city whose architect and builder is God" (John 8:56; Hebrews

11:10). He longed for a better country—a heavenly one (Hebrews 11:16). Abraham received promises of blessing, but it was through Jesus the Messiah that the promises of Jubilee would begin to unfold. Let's turn now to see how Scripture unveils Jesus as the "Ultimate Jubilee."

The Ultimate Jubilee

In the discussion of "70 x 7" earlier, it was noted that Jesus is the fulfillment of the Year of Jubilee. If that is the case, then we should see some proof of that. Lucky for us, there is. When John the Baptist sent his disciples to ask Jesus whether or not he was truly the Messiah, he told them, "Go back and report to John what you hear and see: The blind receive sight, the lame walk, those who have leprosy are cleansed, the deaf hear, the dead are raised, and the good news is proclaimed to the poor" (Matthew 11:4–5). But wait! There's more. Back in his hometown of Nazareth, Jesus stood in the synagogue and read from the scroll of Isaiah 61:1,

> The Spirit of the Lord is on me, because he has anointed me to proclaim good news to the poor. He has sent me to proclaim freedom for the prisoners and recovery of sight for the blind, to set the oppressed free, to proclaim the year of the Lord's favor.

When he had finished reading from the scroll, Jesus sat down, and said, "*This day is this scripture fulfilled* in your ears" (Luke 4:17–21). This quote from Isaiah 61:1 was the very heart and soul of Jubilee, and Jesus is telling them, "I am its fulfillment." It nearly cost him his life, and had he read the next verse, "And *the day of vengeance* of our God," he might not have had to wait for the Romans to crucify him.

Interestingly, Scofield's footnote on Luke 4:19 attributes Jesus stopping at "To proclaim the year of the Lord's favor," and omitting, "The day of vengeance of our God," not because it was dangerous, but because he thinks Jesus is speaking about two separate events, separated by nearly 2,000 years. The "day of vengeance," according to Scofield, belongs to the *second* advent and judgment. Here are a few passages that are contrary to Scofield's footnote on Luke 4:19:

> Therefore, *this generation will be held responsible* for the blood of all the prophets that has been shed since the beginning of the world ... Yes, I tell you, t*his generation will be held responsible* for it all.
>
> –Luke 11:50–51

> *They will not leave one stone on another,* because you did not recognize the time of God's coming to you.
>
> –Luke 19:44 (cf. Matthew 24:2; Mark13:2)

> Truly I say to you; *All these things shall come upon this generation.* O Jerusalem, Jerusalem, who kills the prophets ... how often I wanted to gather your children together, even as a hen gathers her chicks under her wings, and you were unwilling. *Behold, your house is being left to you desolate.*
>
> –Matthew 23:36–38

The early church was about to go through a time of severe testing and persecution unlike anything the world had seen. One generation after Jesus spoke those words in Matthew 23, Jerusalem would be leveled and plowed under—unrecognizable. Jesus had warned his disciples, "Not one stone will be left upon another." He was saying, in effect, that Jerusalem had become a "leprous city."† This was the method of dealing with leprosy prescribed in Leviticus 14:39–45. If, after seven days, the priest still found signs of leprosy in a house that

Steering Off Course

had already been cleansed for that disease, then a persistent defiling mold was said to exist, and the only remedy was to tear the house down—its stones, its timbers, and all the plaster was taken out of the town to an unclean place.

Jesus is saying, in effect, that Jerusalem must receive the same treatment for spreading the "leprosy" of unbelief, for rejecting the very one God had sent to be their salvation. It is for this reason that Partial Fulfillment advocates, such as myself, believe that the book of Revelation was written to first-century Christians about to enter a time of great distress. John begins and ends the book of Revelation with the admonition, "To show the servants of Jesus what must *soon* take place (*táchei*) ... because the time is *near* (*engús*)." The LORD, by inspiring John to remind his readers at the end of Revelation, reusing the bookends "soon" and "near," places the target of his message squarely on the back of the first-century Church.[27] Why else place such temporal restraints as "soon" and "at hand" if the prophecy is of no consequence to the Church for more than 2,000 years? That would make no sense. Nor would it be much comfort.

I highly recommend reading the book of Revelation as John's expanded version of the Olivet Discourse, written within a few years of the destruction of Jerusalem.[28] John was the beloved disciple of Jesus. It only makes sense that he would divulge such important information as the survival of the early Church to his most beloved friend. To hear that God is going to "seal" his Church for protection prior to the pouring out of his wrath on Jerusalem would

---

[27] The temporal restraints "soon" (*tachei*) and "near," or "at hand" *(engus)*, are found in Revelation 1:1,3 and in the final chapter 22:6,7,10,12.

[28] Liberal theologians, who do not believe in prophecy, miracles, or the supernatural in general, push for a late date of writing, A.D. 90-95, in order to eliminate the prophetic nature of the Olivet Discourse. A date of ~A.D. 66 fits the historical record more accurately; the temple was still standing, and Nero, the first emperor to persecute Christians on a wide scale, was still living. He died on 9 June 68.

be a great comfort and source of encouragement when persecution struck. Try reading the book of Revelation from this perspective, and perhaps, for the first time, this difficult book will begin to make sense to you. It is hard to make sense any other way.

We exposed the Gap as one of the legs of the "toothpick foundation" of Futurist teaching. Let us now turn to the other leg—the Prince/Ruler of verse twenty-six.

CHAPTER 4:
Antichrist vs. Jesus Christ

After the sixty-two "sevens," the Anointed One will be put to death and will have nothing. *The people of the prince* who will come will destroy the city and the sanctuary. The end will come like a flood: War will continue until the end, and desolations have been decreed.

He will confirm a covenant with many for one "seven." In the middle of the "seven" he will put an end to sacrifice and offering. And at the temple he will set up an abomination that causes desolation, until the end that is decreed is poured out on him (Daniel 9:26–27).

A new figure is introduced, according to Futurist teaching, in verse 26 of Daniel's vision. He is mentioned in the phrase, "The people of the Prince ..." Futurists claim that the "he" in verse 27 refers to that Prince/Ruler of verse 26. In an effort to strengthen their argument, they claim that this "he" will make a covenant with the Jews. There are a couple of problems with this. First, the rules of grammar have to be dismissed.[29] It can't be referring back to "the people" or the pronoun would be "they" in verse 27. The only antecedent for "he" that fits is "the Anointed One." Second, the Hebrew word used here means "to confirm" or "cause to prevail" (from the root *gabar*). If the text intended to mean

---

[29] The antecedent of a pronoun cannot be the object of a modifying clause.

a covenant was being *made,* one of the common words for "make" or "do" would have been used.³⁰ Did Jesus confirm a covenant? Absolutely! You affirm it every time you celebrate the Eucharist. Luke 22:20 states, "In the same way, after the supper he took the cup, saying, '*This cup is the new covenant in my blood*, which is poured out for you.'"

The vast expanse between interpretations can't get much farther apart than Antichrist and Jesus Christ. The dichotomy here is glaring. The two paths separate like East from West, like "666" from "888." What do I mean by this? Let's check it out.

666 vs. 888

666

Most people are familiar with the phrase, "Mark of the Beast," represented by the number "666." It is found in Revelation 13:16–18. Less well known is that the numerical value of the name Jesus in Greek is "888." Early manuscripts of Revelation 13:18 depict the number "666" using three Greek letters: χ ξ ς. All three letters begin with a "hissing" sound and have the appearance of snakes.³¹ The first of these letters looks like two serpents crossing, the second like a writhing serpent, and the third like a striking serpent. When Moses cast his staff before Pharaoh, what did it turn into—a scorpion or a crocodile? No, a serpent. Why the obsession with serpents? Ah—it hearkens back to the Garden of Eden. It was the serpent who was responsible for the Fall of man. As a result, God negatively transformed the serpent into a creature cursed to eat dust by crawling

---

[30] *Asah* or *poal* (do or make), *bara* (create), or, frequently, the word *karat* was used to refer to the "cutting" of a covenant.

[31] χ ξ ς are pronounced *hexakosioi, hexakonta, hex.*

on its belly. God then added to the curse in pronouncing what has proven to be the fountainhead of all prophecy:

> Because you have done this, I will put enmity between you and the woman, and between your offspring and hers; *he will crush your head*, and you will strike his heel. –Genesis 3:14–15

Listed below are the Greek letters and their values for 666 and 888:

χ	ξ	ς'		Ι	η	σ	ο	υ	ς
600	**60**	**6**		**10**	**8**	**200**	**70**	**400**	**200**

Anyone in the medical or dental field can tell you what the symbol is for their profession—a serpent wound about a staff. This symbol is borrowed from Numbers 21 where the people of Israel were being bitten and killed by venomous vipers. God directed Moses to construct a serpent of bronze and place it on a pole so that anyone looking upon the serpent, shining brightly in the desert sun, would be healed. Moses not only provided us with our legal system, he gave us the symbol for the healing professions. The Israelites knew from the substitutionary sacrifices that were laid upon the altar that brass or bronze signified judgment. The image of the serpent would remind the Jews of the cursed serpent of the Garden, and the brass would let them know that the serpent was already judged in the eyes of God.

For Christians, this image also looks forward to the time when their Messiah, Jesus, would be placed upon a pole. Unlike the serpent, however, he would undeservedly take upon himself all the curse for sin, at least for those who would look to him for their salvation. In both instances, it was pure grace on God's part that led to deliverance. Jesus' own words make the connection, "Just as Moses lifted up the snake in the wilderness, so the Son of Man must

be lifted up, that everyone who believes may have eternal life in him" (John 3:14–15; see also 12:32).

How do you suppose the "Mark of the Beast" became associated with the number "666," or more accurately, 600, 60, and 6? This very number was used long before the Book of Revelation. It is recorded that the weight of the gold that King Solomon received yearly was 666 talents—every year (for how many years we do not know).[32] This is roughly twenty-five tons of gold, valued today at more than $1,300,000,000.00—every year! The number "666" became a fearful sign of apostasy for Israel, as Solomon, the wisest ruler of all, fell prey to disobedience. King Solomon violated all three of the "Big No-No's" that Deuteronomy 17 warned the kings of Israel not to fall prey to:

Warnings

1. Deuteronomy 17:16—The king, moreover, must not acquire great numbers of *horses* ...
2. Deuteronomy 17:17—Neither shall he take many *wives*, or his heart will be led astray.
3. Deuteronomy 17:17—He must not accumulate large amounts of *silver and gold.*

Violations

1. 1 Kings 10:26—Solomon accumulated chariots and horses; he had ... twelve thousand horses.
2. 1 Kings 11:1—King Solomon, however, loved many foreign women ...
3. 1 Kings 10:14—The weight of the gold that Solomon received yearly was 666 talents.

Solomon is the perfect example of how the wisdom of man can quickly turn into foolishness. Matters haven't changed over time, as the apostle Paul admonished the church in Corinth, "Has not God

---

[32] 1 Kings 10:14; 2 Chronicles 9:13.

made foolish the wisdom of the world?" (1 Corinthians 1:20). All of the wisdom of Solomon could not keep the kingdom of Israel from splitting apart. Once the Israel-Judah schism happened, the nation fell into a downward spiral rather quickly. The northern kingdom of Israel disappeared first, captured and absorbed by the Assyrians in 722 B.C. Unrepentant Judah fell prey to king Nebuchadnezzar of Babylon in 586 B.C. Daniel's vision of the 490 years picks up seventy years after that date. The number "666" continues as a fearful reminder for Christians living today to remain diligent against apostasy.

What is the chance that the use of "666" in Revelation 13 is just a coincidence? Right—slim and none. The contrast between "666" and "888" is not accidental. The number "666" represents mankind continually falling short of the divine number 7. It represents the totality of man's failure to resist Satan's temptation in the Garden, "You shall be as gods." The other, "888," represents the superabundance that is to be found in the Lord Jesus Christ.

888

You might expect the value of Jesus' name to be the three-fold sacred number "777," but Jesus was not just about abundance; he was about *superabundance*.[33] The kind of life that Jesus offers is not the typical existence-type of life, *bios*, but life that is abundant and full, *zōē*. People who "come to Christ" are often immediately given a new set of rules to keep, a form of *bios*. These rules invariably focus on the negatives—"Don't do this, don't do that." An old, overripe banana has life in it. A dead fish can still travel downstream. Even a rotting carcass has "life" in it—and it smells bad. But Christians are intended to live from Holy Spirit transformation, and it is about positive action, doing—*zōē*. Hence, the imperatives,

---

[33] Jesus declared in John 10:10, "I came that they might have life *(zōēn)*, and that they might have it more abundantly."

"Love your neighbor," "Be holy," etc. The number "666," by contrast, represents all that is the opposite of love. It represents the lust of the flesh, the lust of the eyes, and the pride of life—all those worldly things the serpent tempted Eve with in the Garden of Eden, and which John warns us of in his epistle, "Come not from the Father but from the world" (1 John 2:16). The number "888" seems to combine in one figure the concept of the Trinity, the number three, and the symbol for infinity, ∞. Infinity stands for something without measure, something that is everlasting. The origin of ∞ can be traced to the everlasting blood covenant that God made with Abraham in Genesis 15. There it is said that God made a covenant by "passing between the pieces" of the split sacrifice in the form of smoke and fire. This movement between the pieces would result in a "figure 8" pattern, similar to the symbol for infinity. The infinity symbol, turned vertically, looks like the number 8. Perhaps the 888-value of Jesus' name is meant to depict the Three-in-One personality and the everlasting nature of God. Just a thought.

    Neither "666" nor "888" is a coincidence. God was in control of the language and the numerical system from the beginning of time. The fact that those letters yielded those numbers only goes to prove that Jesus is, and always has been, greater than Satan. "888" beats "666" every time.

CHAPTER 5:

Pin the Tail on the Antichrist

What do we know about Antichrist? Is it a person? A spiritual attitude? Where is he/it from? Speculations as to the identity of the supposed Antichrist have swirled around in the heads of Apocalypse-obsessed individuals for centuries.[34] Topping the list of the most popular, or at least the most likely, candidate among Protestants is the Pope. Reformation leaders unanimously pointed at the Pope, or the system of the Papacy, as the scriptural Antichrist. Emperor Napoleon was also high on the list. Candidates for Antichrist in the last generation included Hitler, Benito Mussolini, Henry Kissinger, and Mikhail Gorbachev.[35] Nearly every American President since FDR has had their name thrown into the hat.[36] More recent candidates include Emmanuel Macron, the President of France, and Recep Erdogan, President of Turkey. Real creative minds have stirred up concern about the "Idol Shepherd" of Zechariah 11:17 and the mysterious "Assyrian" of Isaiah 10. Still others speculate the Antichrist will be an individual with ties to the Israelite tribe of Dan, based on a single, out-of-

---

[34] The word apocalypse actually means "unveiling" or "revealing," but today most people use Apocalypse in the sense of all things "end of the world."

[35] For younger readers, Soviet Premier Mikhail Gorbachev had a large birthmark on his forehead that reminded Antichrist seekers of the "mark of the beast" or the "mortal wound that had been healed" from Revelation 13.

[36] The exceptions being Jimmy Carter and Gerald Ford, who were not perceived as leaders posing any threat. FDR refers to Franklin Delano Roosevelt, who served as the 32nd president of the United States from 1933 until his death in 1945.

context verse:

> Dan will be a snake by the roadside, a viper along the path, that bites the horse's heels so that its rider tumbles backward.
> —Genesis 49:17

I'm not making this stuff up. There is a new "pin the tail on the Antichrist" figure every month! Anyone who's name can be made to add up to "666" is fair game (sure glad I only have four letters in my middle name!). Don't believe it? Check out Appendix B where I show that even Barney the dinosaur is not safe! Silly? Yes. But that is what much of modern-day Christian eschatology has devolved to, and it will only stop when people like you actually challenge faulty interpretations based on footnotes.

The "number of the beast" that people are advised to calculate in Revelation 13:18 is not 6,6,6, but 600, 60, and 6. Many scholars believe John's first-century audience would quickly recognize this number as a numerical reference to Emperor Nero. Nero was a "beast" of the first order.[37] Many of his exploits are too offensive to print. He murdered his own pregnant wife and had his mother put to death for starters. The term "Roman candle" stems from the Nero era, as the vile emperor took perverse pleasure in watching Christians, wrapped in animal skins, ignited and torched. Compelling evidence for Nero (besides fitting within the one generation time restraint of Jesus' pronouncement in the Olivet Discourse) is the numerical calculation of his name.

John did not record a number that a Roman official scanning Revelation for subversive content could work out in Greek.[38] The most convincing solution to the calculation mystery is that John is

---

[37] Beast doesn't begin to describe Nero. See Edward Champlin, *Nero*, (London: The Belknap Press of Harvard University Press, 2003), or simply search "Nero" online for a quick review of his unspeakable exploits.

[38] Chilton, *Days of Vengeance,* 350.

using a fairly common Hebraic practice called gematria. Gematria consists of calculating the identity of a person or object based on the combined numerical values of each individual letter in the name. Those who understood Hebrew would have little difficulty determining that he was speaking of Nero. Dr. Bruce Metzger, noted New Testament scholar, wrote, "The Greek form 'Neron Caesar' written in Hebrew characters (נרון קסר) is equivalent to 666, whereas the Latin form 'Nero Caesar' (נרו קסר) is equivalent to 616, a textual variant found in a few ancient manuscripts.[39]

ר	ס	ק		ן	ו	ר	נ	
200	60	100		50	6	200	50	= 666

It seems reasonable to conclude John had gematria in mind when he informed his readers to "*calculate* the number of the beast," since he was Jewish and wrote in a Semitic style.[40] It is highly unlikely that John expected his contemporary readers to figure out the name of some 20th-century official in a foreign government.[41] That still holds for the 21st century. "So what?" you might ask. Great question. Fighting over the identity of "666" may not be of much practical value to most people living today. It did, however, make a significant difference to anyone suffering under intense persecution in the generation following Jesus' crucifixion. That knowledge is also helpful to anyone hoping to understand what Revelation was all about. We need to keep Christians who are burdened by State-

---

[39] Bruce M. Metzger, *A Textual Commentary on the Greek New Testament*, (2nd ed.; Stuttgart: German Bible Society, 1994), 676.

[40] Chilton, *Days of Vengeance*, 350–1. Neron Kesar is the linguistically "correct" Hebrew form, the form found in the Talmud and the rabbinical writings. The variant form of Nero Kesar, 616, is the way it would occur to a Gentile to spell it. Nero was sixth in the Julian line of emperors, fitting Revelation 17:10's "five have fallen, one is" re: the seven kings.

[41] *Ibid*, 350.

controlled oppression in our prayers. Note Saint Peter's admonition, "Be alert and of sober mind ... your enemy the devil prowls around like a roaring lion looking for someone to devour. Resist him, standing firm in the faith, because you know that *the family of believers throughout the world is undergoing the same kind of sufferings*" (1 Peter 5:8–9). Just because we have it "good" in America right now does not mean things will always be this way. Paul offers this warning, "Put on the full armor of God, so that you can take your stand against the schemes of the devil" (Ephesians 6:11). Much of the confusion surrounding the Book of Revelation has to do with the late date of writing ascribed to it by many. The date of writing for the Book of Revelation is so often stated to be A.D. 95 that it is often taken as a "matter of fact." Liberal theologians, who do not believe in prophecy, miracles, or the supernatural, always choose this date, as the prophetic element of Revelation is lost. They and other skeptics then pounce on Jesus' words, "Before this generation passes away, all these things will take place," as if he was mistaken. I do not support them in this.

The Seven Heads on Seven Hills

> This calls for a mind with wisdom. The seven heads are seven hills on which the woman sits. *They are also seven kings. Five have fallen, one is,* the other has not yet come; but when he does come, he must remain for only a little while.
> –Revelation 17:9–10

Numerous scholars argue for an earlier date of writing for the Book of Revelation.[42] They see the book being composed during the reign of Emperor Nero, a few years prior to the destruction of the Temple

---

[42] For a thorough examination of the early date of writing for the Book of Revelation, see Kenneth L Gentry, Jr.'s *Before Jerusalem Fell: Dating the Book of Revelation*, (Tyler, TX: Institute for Christian Economics, 1989).

in A.D. 70. Appealing aspects of this view include: (1) he is one generation after Jesus died; (2) the number of his name fits both 666 and the variant 616; (3) the two primary witnesses of the early Church, Peter and Paul, were both killed in Rome during Nero's reign; (4) he was a "beast" of the first order;[43] (5) his suicide on June 9, A.D. 68 was a "mortal wound" ending the Julian line of emperors; (6) he was sixth in line, coming after five emperors had fallen, and the one coming after him, Galba, reigned for only two months (as per 17:10); (7) the tumultuous *Year of the Four Emperors* that followed Nero's death added further credence to the fear that Rome was in its death knell; (8) the Empire was "resurrected" in the Flavian line of emperors when Vespasian rose to power, after the very brief, insignificant reigns of what I call the three "Horns"—Galba, Otho, and Vitellius, who were all lopped off in the span of little more than a year. These three "horns," combined with the seven heads having one horn each, equals the total of the symbolic seven-headed, ten-horned beast.[44]

It was this Beast of Rome that the Jewish religious leaders joined forces with in order to crucify the Lord Jesus Christ during the reign of the Roman Emperor Tiberius. John 18:31 records the words of Pilate to the Jews after they had conducted an illegal trial of Jesus in the middle of the night, "Take him yourselves and judge him according to your law." The Jews replied, "But we have no right to execute anyone." Figuratively, the Harlot had hopped on the back of the Beast to kill the Lamb.

---

[43] Nero was a "beast" of the first order; his perverse exploits are too fowl to print. He kicked his pregnant wife to death and tried multiple times to kill his own mother! The name Nero became proverbial for every kind of despicable behavior imaginable—murder, rape, sodomy, incest, and horrific cruelty, especially to Christians. He persecuted the Christians for 42 months, from November of 64 until his suicide on June 9, 68.

[44] Galba was the seventh *king* but just a horn and not a head. The empire was reborn in the seventh *head* Vespasian, who sent his son Titus, one like unto the seven, to finish off the destruction of Jerusalem in A.D. 70.

There is no consensus on the identity of the seven kings. Partial Fulfillment advocates believe these seven kings point to the order of Roman Emperors beginning with Julius Caesar. Futurists prefer to identify these seven kings as *kingdoms*, most commonly: (1) Egypt, (2) Assyria, (3) Babylon, (4) Media-Persia, (5) Greece, (6) the old Roman Empire, and (7) the future kingdom of Antichrist in a revived Roman Empire. In the table below, I have included my own interpretation of Revelation 17's Seven Heads and Ten Horns in chronological order, where Rome is the *primary* referent of the symbolic number 666, reinforced by the number of the reigning emperor Nero. I would be interested to hear comments on my interpretation and am open to other views.

Five Kings Have Fallen

1. Julius Caesar

2. Caesar Augustus

3. Tiberius

4. Caligula

5. Claudius

    One Is
    6. Nero

        3 "Horns" †
          -Galba
          -Otho
          -Vitellius

            7th Head
            Vespasian

                  8th King; of the 7
                  Titus; A.D. 70

Pin the Tail on the Antichrist

What we do know about antichrist from Scripture is rather limited. The term antichrist is only used five times in four verses:

> Dear children, this is the last hour; and as you have heard that the *antichrist* is coming, even now many *antichrists* have come. This is how we know it is the last hour.
> —1 John 2:18

> Who is the liar? It is whoever denies that Jesus is the Christ. Such a person is the *antichrist*—denying the Father and the Son.
> —1 John 2:22

> Every spirit that does not acknowledge Jesus is not from God. This is the spirit of the *antichrist*, which you have heard is coming and even now is already in the world.
> —1 John 4:3

> I say this because many deceivers, who do not acknowledge Jesus Christ as coming in the flesh, have gone out into the world. Any such person is the deceiver and the *antichrist*.
> —2 John 7

We gather from these four verses that the "spirit of antichrist" entails denying that Jesus is the Son of God, come in the flesh. What we do *not* glean from these texts is any notion of an individual superpower Antichrist coming in the future. Note: that does not exclude the *possibility* that, as Satan gathers the forces of evil against God's saints, an individual all-powerful sovereign might be inaugurated over a New World Order, but it also does not mean we should obsess over this potential possibility. After all, who really believes our own presidents are running things on their own today? John points out, *many antichrists* (plural) were already active in the first century! There is also no mention of a seven-year tribulation connected with antichrist. That notion is not found in Daniel's vision either. It is, however, *derived* from there. Ingenious yes; but accurate? No! Not one of the "proof texts" of Dispensational teaching says a word about a seven-year tribulation. Here is the list of their most popular go-to proof texts:

Ezekiel 38–39	Gog and Magog
Matthew 24:21	Great Tribulation
Daniel 7:1–7	7-headed, 10-horned beasts (parallels in Revelation 13;17)
1 Thessalonians 4:15–17	The Rapture
2 Thessalonians 2:1–12	Man of Lawlessness
Revelation 13:16–18	Mark of the Beast

Futurists can talk all they want about these interesting events or characters, but, in order to come up with the key element in their system, the seven-year tribulation, they must go back to the ninth chapter of Daniel. The "Gap" and the Prince of their seven-year Great Tribulation provide the ultra-slim foundation upon which Futurist prophetic interpretation rests. That is why I often refer to it as a "toothpick" foundation.

    A few comments need to be made in reference to a couple of the "proof texts" listed above. Ezekiel 38–39 is frequently used by Futurists to suggest a coming war involving Russia, based on the use of the Hebrew term *ro'sh*. Though there is a phonetic similarity between the two words *ro'sh* and Russia, it does not mean, nor ever has meant Russia. *Ro'sh* is a common Old Testament word, used more than 600 times. It means "head" or "chief." It is unlikely that in this one instance its meaning changed to "Russia." The same goes for other phonetically similar names like Tubal for Tobolsk and Meshech for Moscow. Christian writer Ralph Woodrow pointed out, "Some think Gomer means Germany. It is true the words 'Gomer'

Pin the Tail on the Antichrist

and 'Germany' both begin with a 'G.' So does guess-work. The words Heaven and Hell both begin with the letter 'H,' but this does not make them the same place!"[45]

Ezekiel 38–39 was not about modern warfare against Israel in the future, as evidenced by the use of primitive weapons (spears, bow and arrow, etc., 38:4,5; 39:9), all the riders in the battle are riding on horses (38:15), the people of Israel are said to be dwelling in safety (38:11), and the invasion is for the purpose of obtaining silver, gold, and cattle! No mention of oil. Speaking of oil, it was a slick move on the part of John Walvoord, former president of Dallas Theological Seminary, when he republished his 1974 book, *Armageddon, Oil, and the Middle East Crisis*, during the Gulf War in Iraq in 1991. The conflict was over in days, however, and his book sales slipped fast.[46] Based on the details of the battle depicted in Ezekiel, it is more likely a description of either the people of Israel's fight for survival due to Haman's treachery in the book of Esther or the revolt waged by the Maccabees against Antiochus Epiphanes IV from 167–160 B.C.[47]

The Man of Lawlessness of 2 Thessalonians 2 is another one of those passages made difficult by projecting this mysterious figure into the future. Whoever he is, keep in mind that the apostle Paul had warned the citizens of Thessalonica of the possibility that *they* may hear of the "Coming of the Lord" *by letter,* therefore, it cannot be

---

[45] Ralph Woodrow, *His Truth Is Marching On: Advanced Studies on Prophecy in the Light of History*, (Riverside, CA: Ralph Woodrow Evangelistic Association, Inc., 1977), 41.

[46] *Armageddon, Oil and the Middle East Crisis* cashed in big time when it was dug out of moth balls just before the 1991 Gulf war and sold over 1.5 million copies. Bummer for him, the war only lasted for a few days or he may have outsold Hal Lindsey.

[47] For compelling arguments for the fulfillment of Ezekiel 38-39 in the events of the book of Esther, see: Gary Demar, *The Gog and Magog End-Time Alliance: Israel, Russia, and Syria in Bible Prophecy* (Powder Springs, GA: American Vision Press, 2016), 55-60, or, James B. Jordan, *Esther in the Midst of Covenant History* (Niceville, FL: Biblical Horizons, 1995), 5-7.

referring to the end of the space-time universe.[48] It makes sense, if Paul taught in Thessalonica about Jesus' speech concerning Jerusalem (which seems likely), he would point out that since Jerusalem had not yet fallen, then the Second Coming obviously hadn't happened yet. The destruction of Jerusalem will precede the Second Coming according to the Olivet Discourse. It is important to study the significance of the fall of Jerusalem to Jesus and Paul. One risks falling into the trap of over-complicating matters when avoiding the context and ... historical facts. Paul says to his first-century listeners, "You *know* what restrains him" (the man of lawlessness; 2:6). We can't say that today.

Speculation about the Mark of the Beast and how it will manifest itself in modern times has filled countless volumes in recent decades. Eligibility for the fulfillment of the "mark" is almost as prevalent as candidates for the Antichrist. Credit cards, grocery store scanners, and, more recently, Covid-19 vaccines have topped the list of "marks" that the State wants to place on its citizens. Revelation 13 describes a political beast rising from the sea and a second religious beast (it looks like a lamb but speaks like a dragon; 13:11) coming out of the land. All who refuse to worship the image of the first beast are to be killed. None of the people administering vaccines or scanning credit cards for payment have demanded any form of worship as yet, so I think we are still safe. The LORD commanded the people of Israel to bind his words on their hand or forehead as far back as Exodus 13:9 and the first Passover (cf. Deuteronomy 6:8; 11:18). He wanted them to be intentional about passing on the faith to their children using the visual reminder of little boxes of Scripture tied on their hand or forehead. These boxes are called phylacteries, and they contained four portions of the Law (Exodus 13:2–10;

---

[48] N. T. Wright, *The New Testament and the People of God*, (Minneapolis: Fortress Press, 1992), 460.

Exodus 13:11–16; Deuteronomy 6:4–9; and Deuteronomy 11:13–21).

The LORD had one of his messengers mark (Hebrew *tav*) the foreheads of the godly citizens of Jerusalem prior to sending forth executioners into the city to slay the unmarked wicked in Ezekiel 9. In ancient Hebrew, this sign, *tav*, was composed of two symbols—a cross and a nail![49] Thousands of years before Jesus died on the cross, a sign for covenant with God appeared in the form of the *tav* on the forehead. Revelation 14:1 speaks of the Lamb on Mt. Zion standing with the 144,000 who had been previously sealed on the forehead from the twelve tribes of Israel (7:2–4).[50] The curse in Genesis 3 had as one of its negative consequences the sweat on the brow (forehead), hence the priests were clothed in vegetables (linen) rather than in animals (wool); they were forbidden to wear the skins of beasts, because they produced *sweat* (Ezekiel 44:17–18; cf. Genesis 3:19).[51]

The Lord Jesus Christ

Returning to our metaphorical Continental Divide, let's check out the slopes on the other side so that we can clearly see just how profound the expanse between camps is when it comes to the kingdom of God. The view from this vantage point reveals Jesus initiating his Father's kingdom and ushering in the New Covenant. God sent John the Baptist to proclaim his cousin Jesus as the Messiah; "Repent, for the kingdom of heaven has come near"

---

[49] Dr. Frank T. Seekins, *Hebrew Word Pictures: How Does The Hebrew Alphabet Reveal Prophetic Truths?*, (Phoenix: Living Word Pictures Inc.: 2003), 32, 35, 96, 99.

[50] The list of twelve tribes of Israel here does not include Dan and Ephraim, who were guilty of idolatry in connection with the golden calves (1 Kings 12:25,28–29). In their place are Levi and Joseph. Judah has replaced Reuben as the firstborn as well. The 144,000 seem to symbolically represent the Jews who first received and accepted the Gospel.

[51] Chilton, *Days of Vengeance*, 279.

(Matthew 3:2; Malachi 3:1). John was imprisoned shortly after he baptized Jesus, where, upon his anointing, a dove descended upon the Savior signaling the birth of a new spiritual world (Luke 3:22).[52] Jesus picked up where the Baptizer left off, "From that time on Jesus began to preach, 'Repent, for the kingdom of heaven has come near'" (Matthew 4:17). Hints that God's kingdom had actually arrived in Jesus were evident in the many miraculous healings he was performing. "Could this be the Son of David?" the people began asking. Even those who opposed Jesus could not deny what the people, and their own eyes, were telling them. So, they turned to a different strategy. Thinking that Jesus was a false prophet, they accused him of performing miracles at the bequest of the prince of demons—Beelzebul.[53] It is at this point that Jesus makes one of the most well-known and powerful statements in regards to God's kingdom:

> But if I cast out demons by the Spirit of God, then *my kingdom has come* upon you.
> –Matthew 12:24–28

Don't miss that last line—"Then my kingdom has come upon you." Jesus certainly *did* cast out demons. Even the Pharisees could see that. So, unless you want to side with the Pharisees, the logical conclusions are: (1) that Jesus did indeed cast out demons by the power of the Holy Spirit; and (2) this was proof that his kingdom had come. Jesus is "binding the strong man" in order to plunder his house. He is boldly declaring that he is the fulfillment of Isaiah 49:24–26:

---

[52] Compare Genesis 8:10–12 where a dove was lighting upon a renewed physical world.

[53] The actual name of the demon is Beelzebub, "lord of the flies." The Jewish leaders, intending to ridicule Jesus, used the more derogatory Beelzebul, "lord of the dung."

> Can plunder be taken from warriors, or captives be rescued from the fierce? But this is what the LORD says: *Yes, captives will be taken from warriors, and plunder retrieved from the fierce*; I will contend with those who contend with you, and your children I will save ... Then all mankind will know that I, the LORD, am your Savior, your Redeemer, the Mighty One of Jacob.

Futurists appear to side with the Pharisees here. This was early in his ministry, they say, but once he was rejected, then God's kingdom had to be deferred. One post-resurrection quote from Jesus should put that argument to bed,

> All authority has been given to me, in heaven and on earth.
> –Matthew 28:18

It does not say, "Some authority has been given to me," or, "Authority has been given to me in heaven." No, this is an all-inclusive authority. How does this fit with the Futurist teaching about Jesus receiving an earthly reign, in Jerusalem, for 1,000 years? Not very well. Jesus' authority is everlasting; his sovereignty is over all (2 Samuel 7:13,16; Psalm 72:17; 89:3–4; Ezekiel 37:25). Conveniently (for them), other than those who set specific dates for Christ's Return and failed, speculation about future events cannot be disproved.

Paul's bold statement in Ephesians 1:19–21 could not be made if Jesus were not, in fact, reigning with authority now:

> That power is the same as the mighty strength he exerted *when he raised Christ from the dead, and seated him at his right hand* in the heavenly realms, far above all rule and authority, power and dominion,

and every name that is invoked, *not only in the present age but also in the one to come.*

The phrase "seated him at his right hand" is highly significant. The Olivet Discourse contains the statement "then will appear the sign of the Son of Man in heaven." Whereas Futurists claim this is talking about some awe-inspiring *sign in the skies* that will signal Jesus' imminent Return, others believe that the visible, terrible events that befell Jerusalem in A.D. 70 *were the sign* that Jesus is now seated in the heavens. This second interpretation is evidenced by the martyrdom of Stephen.

The Church's first martyr, Stephen, saw a vision just before he died, saying to the stirred-up crowd, "Look!" "I see heaven open, and the Son of Man *standing* at the right hand of God" (Acts 7:56). It is as if he sees Jesus getting up off his throne in order to greet him! What a powerful image. What an encouraging picture for someone about to die, but also for anyone struggling with their own difficult day-to-day circumstances. That is an image any believer can look forward to—Jesus standing and waiting to greet them when their turn comes. I can get excited about that! Sounds like Stephen did too. Hear these closing words of Acts 7:

> While they were stoning him, Stephen prayed, Lord Jesus, receive my spirit. Then he fell on his knees and cried out, *Lord, do not hold this sin against them.* When he had said this, he fell asleep.
>
> –Acts 7:59–60

Wow! Powerful stuff. Where have we heard that before? At the foot of the cross, when Jesus said, "Father, forgive them, for they do not know what they are doing" (Luke 23:34). Those words of grace from the parched lips of a thoroughly exhausted Jesus led to the salvation of one of the criminals being executed next to him; his eleventh-hour defense of Jesus' innocence opened the doors of Paradise for him. "Father, forgive them, for they do not know what they are doing."

May those words of grace apply to us for our sorry failures when it comes to interpreting difficult passages of Scripture. Since actions have consequences, when it comes to our efforts at interpretation, we have an extremely important decision to make—are we going to be biblical or speculative? That is the mantle we will now pick up.

CHAPTER 6:

The Flight of the Speculative Spaceship

Apologetics refers to defense of one's faith. Greg Bahnsen, the late Christian apologist, argued that believers should be able to show religious contenders where their worldviews will lead them. He was talking about non-believers and their worldviews, but this same method ought to be applied to eschatological interpretations. What are the consequences of your belief? Where does your belief lead you? This goes for all sides. Bahnsen would say of non-Christian worldviews, "Once you 'get on that flight,' there is no getting off."[54] Fortunately, having a difference of opinion on how to interpret a prophetic text is not on the same level as one's salvation. There are alternative "flights" available for us to board. Let's compare the Futurist and Partial Fulfillment viewpoints and see where they take us.

Futurist/Dispensational Viewpoint

One of the consequences of boarding the Futurist "flight" is a totally different take on the "Last Days." Some of you may have noticed in the passage about many antichrists, from 1 John 2:18, that John finished by saying, "This is how we know *it is the last hour*." We know he wasn't talking about the "End of the World" (people would have noticed!). What, then, was John talking about? Well, Futurism, as the name implies, applies "last days" to our future, to the time of their Great Tribulation. A majority of Futurists see May 14, 1948, the date of Israel's independence, as signaling that we are living in

---

[54] Bahnsen, Greg, *Defending the Christian Worldview,* Disc 8.

the last days. They see the last days as referring to the end of what Scofield labels the "Church Age." The most important features for the Dispensational system are: (1) the "seven dispensations," and (2) a pre-tribulation rapture of the church prior to their coming seven-year tribulation. The *pre-tribulation* rapture view is not an essential doctrine of Dispensationalism, as many believe in a pre-wrath, mid-tribulation rapture and others in a post-tribulation rapture. For them, the "Day of the LORD" is the time when God's judgment will be poured out on an unbelieving world and Israel will be saved and restored. This "flight" takes us to a future earthly reign of Jesus in Jerusalem, where Israel will perform a functional role to the nations.

If you were to ask a Futurist whether they believe Jesus could "come again at any moment," 99% would shout an emphatic "Yes!" Ah, but that is not the case if you reside in the Great Tribulation camp. Remember—there are consequences for our beliefs. A whole slew of things must happen first: (1) a revived Roman Empire (usually in the form of a European Union); (2) a rebuilt temple; (3) a new priesthood; (4) animal sacrifices; (5) an individual to arise and rule; and (6) a New World Order. All this because of adherence to a strict literal interpretation that does not treat the Bible as normal literature. This "one-size-fits-all" approach negates Scripture's use of poetry, symbols, the metaphorical, etc. It then skews our vision and the methods with which we approach other apocalyptic passages. Messages intended for the early Church get pushed thousands of years into the future and thousands of miles away from any practical purpose for its first-century audience. The Book of Revelation and verses about the "last days" are perfect examples. Apparently *our* generation is more important than anyone else.

Partial Fulfillment Viewpoint

Rather than the "last days" referring to our generation, or one even further down the line, the Partial Fulfillment view sees them as a description of the last days of the old covenant. This is not a mere opinion. Nearly all references in the New Testament to the "last days" are referring to the demise of the old covenant. Here are some examples:

> In the past God spoke to our forefathers through the prophets at many times and in various ways, *but in these last days* he has spoken to us by his Son.
> –Hebrews 1:2

> Then Christ would have to suffer many times since the creation of the world. *But now* he has appeared once for all *at the end of the ages* to do away with sin by the sacrifice of himself.
> –Hebrews 9:26

> For you know that it was not with perishable things such as silver or gold that you were redeemed ... but with the precious blood of Christ, a lamb without blemish or defect. He was chosen before the creation of the world, but was revealed *in these last times* for your sake.
> –1 Peter 1:18–20

> These people are not drunk, as you suppose. It's only nine in the morning! *This* [*Pentecost events*] is what was spoken by the prophet Joel: *In the last days*, God says, I will pour out my Spirit on all people.
> –Acts 2:15–17

> These things happened to them as examples and were written down as warnings *for us, on whom the end of the ages has come.*
> –1 Corinthians 10:11

Hebrews 8:13 refers to the old covenant as "obsolete and aging, and about to disappear." This is totally different from the end of time and space, the time of the Final Judgment, which is likened to the days of Noah—"That is how it will be at the coming (*Parousía*) of the Son of Man" (Matthew 24:37–39). When you only see "last" as literally the last days of the world, then this is what you come up with. Picking and choosing texts to fit your narrative leads to rampant inconsistency—to what I call, "literal when convenient." The Olivet Discourse, found in Matthew 24, Mark 13, and Luke 21, is a perfect example of this problem. All three accounts say virtually the same thing. The first few verses of the three Gospel accounts of the Olivet Discourse are provided below. Reading those verses alone, I believe most people would have a hard time seeing how they could be talking about different things. I recommend you take the time to read all three accounts, one after another. Side-by-side comparisons of the three texts are also valuable and can easily be found online. For convenience, here is a partial side-by-side comparison:

The Olivet Discourse

Matthew 24:1–3	**Mark 13:1–4**	**Luke 21:5–7**
Jesus left the temple and was walking away when his disciples came up to him to call his attention to its buildings. "Do you see all these things?" he asked. "Truly I tell you, not one stone here will be left on another; every one will be thrown down." As Jesus was sitting on the Mount of Olives, the disciples came to him privately. "Tell us," they said, "when will this happen, and what	As Jesus was leaving the temple, one of his disciples said to him, "Look, Teacher! What massive stones! What magnificent buildings!" "Do you see all these great buildings?" replied Jesus. "Not one stone here will be left on another; everyone will be thrown down." As Jesus was sitting on the Mount of Olives opposite the temple, Peter, James, John, and Andrew asked him privately, "Tell us, when will	Some of his disciples were remarking about how the temple was adorned with beautiful stones and with gifts dedicated to God. But Jesus said, "As for what you see here, the time will come when not one stone will be left on another; every one of them will be thrown down."

will be the sign of your coming and of the end of the age?"	these things happen? And what will be the sign that they are all about to be fulfilled?"	
v.15–16	**v. 14–15**	**v. 20–21**
So when you see standing in the holy place 'the Abomination that causes desolation,' spoken of by the prophet Daniel—let the reader understand— then let those who are in Judea flee to the mountains.	But when you see standing in the holy place 'the Abomination that causes desolation,' spoken of by the prophet Daniel— let the reader understand— then let those who are in Judea flee to the mountains.	But when you see Jerusalem being surrounded by armies, Then you will know that its desolation is near. Then let those who are in Judea flee to the mountains.

The last two verses posted above will be dealt with in detail in the next chapter. They were placed here merely so that a fair comparison of the three texts can be made as to whether or not they refer to the same topic.

In the Olivet Discourse, beginning with the verses posted above, Jesus warns about false Messiahs, of wars and rumors of war, of famine and earthquakes, but reminds them that the "end" is not yet. Matthew 24:9 states, "Then *you* will be handed over to be persecuted and put to death, and *you* will be hated by all nations because of me." He says that many will turn away from the faith and will betray and hate each other. He warns of many false prophets who will appear and deceive many people, and that because of the increase of wickedness, the love of most will grow cold. Jesus finishes, however, with a high note: "The one who stands firm to the end will be saved; and this gospel of the kingdom will be preached in the whole world as a testimony to all nations, and then the end will come" (Matthew 24:13–14).

Who do you suppose Jesus was referring to when he said, "So when *you* see standing in the holy place 'the Abomination that causes desolation'"? Do you think he was talking to his disciples, or to you and me, in the West, 2,000 years later? Noted New Testament scholar N. T. Wright states, "Mark's note in 13:14 ('let the reader understand') shows (a) that he took the 'abomination' to refer to Roman invasion and (b) that he thought it dangerous to say so explicitly."[55] Wars were rampant in the time between Christ's crucifixion and the fall of Jerusalem. The Jewish Rebellion against Rome began in A.D. 66, three and a half years before Jerusalem's destruction. Earthquakes and famine were a common plague in the Middle East. The famous volcanic eruption of Pompeii and its resultant destruction occurred in A.D. 62, just eight years before the destruction of Jerusalem by a different means—the armies of Rome. Paul was seeking financial relief for the poor of Jerusalem, whose condition was made worse due to famine and earthquake (Galatians 2:10; 2 Corinthians 8). The Olivet Discourse goes on to say,

> Pray that your flight will not take place in winter or on the Sabbath. For then there will be great distress, unequaled from the beginning of the world until now—*and never to be equaled again.*
> –Matthew 24:21–22

Emphasis is placed on the italicized portion of the last verse, because if this really is about the last days of time and space, then this phrase is rendered meaningless. It makes total sense if it refers to the middle of history and the events of A.D. 70, but not in the sense that Futurism uses it. Another claim that is often made is, "The Great Tribulation couldn't have happened yet, because those days of

---

[55] N. T. Wright, *Jesus and the Victory of God*, (Minneapolis: Fortress Press, 1996), 511.

unequaled distress have not occurred." The children whose parents and grandparents were slaughtered by the Roman armies in A.D. 70 might beg to differ. Those who did survive this massacre were hauled off as slaves. A greater percentage of Jews were killed in this first-century Holocaust than died in the 1940s Holocaust under Adolf Hitler. A great tribulation did occur upon Israel, just not the seven-year Great Tribulation Futurists are anticipating. It also occurred within one generation, just as Jesus had warned them it would (Matthew 24:34).

Tale of Two Sieges

Scofield goes so far as to argue that the Olivet Discourse in Matthew and Mark speaks to an entirely different event than that in Luke's account. This should make one curious. If Scofield is going to argue for two sieges of Jerusalem based on Matthew and Mark's use of the word "abomination" where Luke uses the term "armies," then he should also argue for two separate crucifixions. Matthew, Mark, and John all use the Hebrew term *Golgothá* as the site of Jesus' crucifixion; Luke uses a different term—*Kraníon* ("cranium"). Why doesn't Scofield argue for two separate crucifixions based on Luke's use of *Cranium* rather than *Golgotha*?[56] He doesn't because they speak of the same event, just as the Olivet Discourse speaks of one event. Inconsistency once again rules. Here is a direct quote from part of Scofield's footnote on Luke 21:20:

> *Two sieges of Jerusalem are in view* in the Olivet Discourse, the *one fulfilled* in A.D. 70, and *the other yet to be fulfilled* at the end of the age. Here the reference is to the siege by Titus, A.D. 70, when the city was taken and vv. 20–24 literally fulfilled. These horrors illustrated the conditions in Palestine at the

---

[56] *Cranium* (Greek) and *Golgotha* (Hebrew) both mean "Skull." Jerome, writer of the Latin translation of the Bible known as the Vulgate, used *Calvary* for the place of the Skull. Maybe there are three separate crucifixions! I'm joking.

time of the end, but neither v. 20 nor v. 24 is included in the accounts of the Olivet Discourse given by Matthew and Mark.[57]

It is interesting that he singles out the omission of verses 20 and 24 in Matthew and Mark. These are the verses describing the armies attacking Jerusalem and her inhabitants being slaughtered by the sword and its survivors being led away captive. What Scofield does *not* point out, however, is that verse 28 is not mentioned in Matthew or Mark—

> When you see these things begin to come to pass, then look up, and lift up your heads; for your redemption draws near.
> –Luke 21:28

Incredible, since you will hear this verse quoted all the time by Futurists as a "proof text" that the End is near, *as if it were* written in Matthew and Mark! Such cherry-picking of verses in an effort to support one's argument is poor scholarship.

---

[57] C.I. Scofield, *The New Scofield Reference Bible:* King James Version, (New York: Oxford University Press, 1967), 1114.

End Times: "Are We There Yet?"

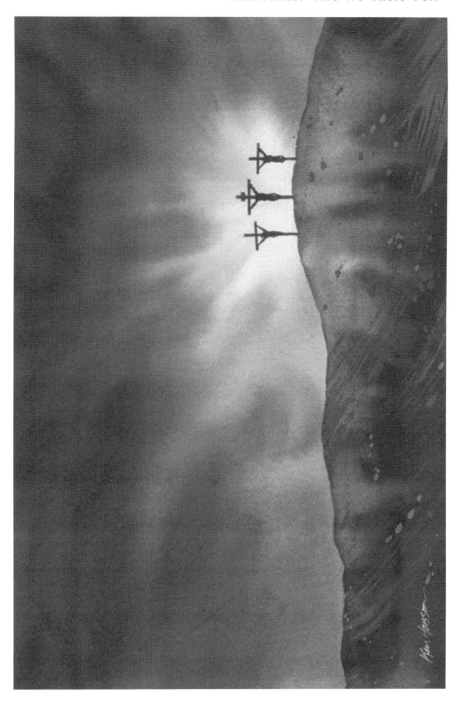

Deceivers and False Christs

In Matthew 24:24, Jesus warns of false messiahs and false prophets who will appear and perform great signs and wonders to deceive, if possible, even the elect. Deceivers and false Christs were running wild in Israel in the first century. The Book of Acts alone mentions four such false messiahs who led astray thousands: Theudas (Acts 5:36); Judas the Galilean (5:37); Simon Magus (8:9); and the Egyptian false prophet (21:38). Emperor Nero had several false prophets killed every day!

The Gospel of the Kingdom Will Be Preached to the Whole World

Another thing you will frequently hear Dispensationalists claim is, "The gospel of the kingdom was not preached to the whole world, so how could it be referring to events of the first century?" Scripture reports that the gospel of the kingdom *was* indeed preached to all the world, for the apostle Paul emphasizes this point at least five times just in his letters to the Romans and Colossians.[58] Here are three such examples:

> First, I thank my God through Jesus Christ for all of you, because your faith is *being reported all over the world*.
> —Romans 1:8

> But I ask: Did they not hear? Of course they did: Their voice has gone out *into all the earth* their words *to the ends of the inhabited earth*.
> —Romans 10:18

---

[58] A fairly comprehensive use of words is used to convey the scope of the Gospel outreach: world (*kosmos*); earth (*gē*); inhabited earth (*oikouménē*); all creation (*pasē ktísei*). See also Romans 16:26 and Colossians 1:6.

> If indeed you continue in the faith firmly established and steadfast, and not moved away from the hope of the gospel that you have heard, *which was proclaimed in all creation under heaven.*
> –Colossians 1:23

The gospel of the kingdom went throughout the inhabited earth, but how did they understand the Olivet Discourse? Did Christians in Israel expect an Antichrist figure to place an idol in their holy Temple, and when that did not happen, they suffered through the trials brought on by the Jewish Rebellion with the attitude "whatever will be will be" or "it must be God's will"? Or, did they prepare for soon-to-come severe trials, ready to flee at a moment's notice when the armies of Rome surrounded the walls of Jerusalem? It was life or death for Christians of the first century. Fortunately for us, it is not a "life or death" matter, but it is extremely important for an understanding of who or what the abomination of desolation is/was. It is time to turn our attention to that matter now.

CHAPTER 7:

The Abomination of Desolation

Matthew 24:15–16	Mark 13:14–15	Luke 21:20–21
So when you see standing in the holy place "the Abomination that causes desolation," spoken of by the prophet Daniel—let the reader understand— then let those who are in Judea flee to the mountains.	But when you see standing in the holy place "the Abomination that causes desolation," spoken of by the prophet Daniel—let the reader understand— then let those who are in Judea flee to the mountains.	But when you see Jerusalem being surrounded by armies, Then you will know that its desolation is near. Then let those who are in Judea flee to the mountains.

Luke is virtually identical to Matthew and Mark, until, that is, you get to the phrase "the abomination of desolation." Luke, remember, is a Gentile, speaking to a Gentile audience. The Jews would have been familiar with Daniel's "abomination that causes desolation," but not the Gentiles. Luke puts this phrase in plain language, "When you see Jerusalem surrounded by armies, then know that it is time to flee to the mountains."

Practically any modern movie, TV program, book, or blog related to "end times" will tell you that a treaty will be made with Israel in the future by a globalist leader for seven years, and that after three and a half years (the "midst of the 'week'"), this global figure will break his treaty with the Jews and begin a world-wide persecution. They believe that the abomination of desolation refers to an idol that will be set up within a currently non-existent temple, by a deceptive Antichrist who is yet to burst upon the scene. The idol will likely be a reproduction of this world leader. Where do they come up with this? The only place in Scripture this *can* be derived from is Daniel 9:26–27. It is by cherry-picking different passages of text and splicing them together that the Futurist is able to connect their Great Tribulation to the Olivet Discourse, as well as The Man of Sin (2 Thessalonians 2), the Mark of the Beast (Revelation 13), the Rapture (1 Thessalonians 4), Gog and Magog (Ezekiel 38–39), and the 1,000 Years (Revelation 20). Yet, not one of those passages says a word about a coming seven-year tribulation. That is why one's interpretation of Daniel's vision is so critical. Interpretations have consequences. Let's step into the murky waters a little deeper.

The Prince and the Covenant

The Ruler/Prince appears for the first time in Daniel's vision in chapter nine, verse twenty-six, as the object of the modifying clause, "The people of the prince."

> After the sixty-two "sevens," the Anointed One will be put to death and will have nothing. *The people of the prince* who will come will destroy the city and the sanctuary. The end will come like a flood: War will continue until the end, and desolations have been decreed.
>
> *He* will confirm a covenant with many for one "seven." In the middle of the "seven" he will put an end to sacrifice and offering. And at the temple he will set up an abomination that causes desolation, until the end that is decreed is poured out on him (9:27).

The Abomination of Desolation

This creates a problem for those who claim that the "he" in the following verse refers to that prince, as a pronoun cannot have as its antecedent (referent) the object of a modifying clause.[59] Grammarians would have your head on a platter. "He" would have to refer back to either one of the subjects, "Anointed One," or "people," but it cannot be referring to "people" or the proper pronoun would be "they." The "Anointed One," messiah, is the only referent that fits the facts both grammatically and historically. Jesus confirmed the New Covenant during the Last Supper. Further, what would be the point of a treaty or covenant that would be in existence for a measly seven years? Numerous treaties have been broken within that time span, but can you think of any treaties specifically designed for a mere seven years?

Almost universally, the argument used by those who are expecting a future Great Tribulation is, "The Great Tribulation *has* to be in the future, because it hasn't happened yet." Really? What do historians have to say? Josephus, first-century Romano-Jewish historian and military leader, recorded in his *The Jewish War* that an estimated 1.1 million were killed in the Jewish War, that 115,880 dead were carried out one of the gates during the month of Nisan in A.D. 70, and that 97,000 were taken as slaves.[60] The seven-year Great Tribulation proposed by Dispensationalism may have not occurred, but to say that great affliction/tribulation (*thlipsis*) did not occur in the first century is flat-out wrong. It was *expected* by the Christians in Jerusalem, as they heeded Jesus' warning and fled the city when they got the chance in A.D. 66. Gessius Florus, the Roman general dispatched by Emperor Nero to deal with the upstart Jewish Zealots, victory within his grasp, inexplicably withdrew his troops, throwing the door open for the Christians to flee. The Believers, trapped within the confines of the city walls, must have stared at

---

[59] Ralph Woodrow, *Great Prophecies*, 111.

[60] Flavius Josephus, *The Wars of the Jews*, (Book VI, Ch. 9, Sec 3).

each other in utter amazement, as it suddenly dawned on them—this was the very thing Jesus had warned us about (Luke 21:20). Without hesitating, they leaped up like the proverbial paralytic, grabbed the dog and kids, and fled to the hillsides.[61]

The Abomination of Desolation

The identity of the abomination of desolation depends on who you listen to. Partial Fulfillment advocates, believing the term refers to armies surrounding Jerusalem, confidently assert that it is a colorful way of depicting that city's utter desolation in A.D. 70. They offer as evidence the scene immediately preceding the Olivet Discourse, where Jesus' disciples are marveling at the magnificent stones and buildings of the temple complex, "Look, Teacher! What massive stones! What magnificent buildings!" Jesus replied, "Not one stone would be left upon another," and he wasn't kidding. The Romans plowed up the ground upon which Jerusalem was built, barely leaving a trace of its former existence. It was as if Jesus had diagnosed Jerusalem as suffering from recurrent leprosy. Once all other methods of treatment had been exhausted, the only alternative, according to Jewish law in Leviticus 14, was to dismantle the entire structure; tear it down and burn it outside the city. All three Gospel writers are narrating the same historic event according to the Partial Fulfillment interpretation.

Futurists assert with equal confidence that, while Luke is talking about the armies destroying Jerusalem in A.D. 70, Matthew and Mark are speaking to events surrounding the Great Tribulation and the 70th Week of Daniel. For them, the Abomination of Desolation (note the use of capital letters, making it about a person

---

[61] N.T. Wright notes that the tradition of Christians getting out of Jerusalem and going to Pella hardly counts as fleeing "to the hills;" to get to Pella they would have to descend 3,000 feet to the Jordan valley and then travel north for about thirty miles ... no one in their right mind would describe a flight to Pella as "to the hills." Wright, *Victory of God*, 353.

or idol) refers to events in our future. It is here that the "Gap" comes in handy. The "Gap" functions as a multi-purpose measuring device I refer to as the Dispensational ruler. A model of a Dispensational ruler works great for demonstrative purposes. Simply cut a short piece off of a normal yardstick and attach that short piece to the remaining long piece using two large rubber bands. The short piece represents the 70th week in Daniel's prophecy. First, you can illustrate the consecutive nature of the Partial Fulfillment view by holding the two pieces together. Second, there is an added bonus—the flexibility of the rubber bands allows you to stretch the 70th week to whatever length you need. It never breaks (at least it hasn't yet), and it allows one to fit any headline or current event, no matter what century you are living in, to fit the desired narrative. This makes for great book sales but lousy scholarship.

The physician Luke, a Gentile, doesn't mince words. He comes right out and tells his non-Jewish audience that the abomination that causes desolation is "the *armies surrounding Jerusalem*." All three Gospel accounts contain Jesus' admonition to flee, but, according to Futurists, Matthew and Mark's audience is purported to be afraid of an idol that is to be mounted in a Temple (cf. Matthew 24:15; Mark 13:14; Luke 21:20). Worth noting—Idols might defile a temple; they do not raise it to the ground. Armies do, and that is exactly what the de-creation language in the Olivet Discourse, as well as some of the Old Testament prophets, points to.[62]

> Immediately after the distress of those days the *sun will be darkened*, and the *moon* will not give its light; the *stars* will fall from the sky, and the heavenly bodies will be shaken.
>
> –Matthew 24:29

---

[62] See also Isaiah 24:23; Jeremiah 15:9; Joel 2:10; Amos 8:9; Acts 2:16–21; 2 Peter 3:7,10–12; Revelation 6:12–14; 16:10.

> See, the day of the Lord is coming—a cruel day, with wrath and fierce anger ... The stars of heaven and their constellations will not show their light. The rising *sun will be darkened and the moon will not give its light.*
>
> –Isaiah 13:9–10

> When I snuff you out, I will cover the heavens and darken their *stars*; I will cover the *sun* with a cloud, and the *moon* will not give its light.
>
> –Ezekiel 32:7

> I will pour out my Spirit in those days. I will show wonders in the heavens and on the earth, blood and fire and billows of smoke. *The sun will be turned to darkness and the moon to blood* before the coming of the great and dreadful day of the Lord.
>
> –Joel 2:29–31

Scary sounding de-creation language—sun darkened, moon turned to blood, stars fallen, etc.—was commonly used in the Old Testament to instill fear and a sense of doom and gloom into the hearts of any nation in the crosshairs of the LORD's wrath. These very nations that were to undergo judgment were, at times, first utilized by God to punish Israel for her sins. Egypt, Assyria, Babylon, Persia, and Syria all had their turns. The image of the LORD *"coming on the clouds"* was used to depict the judgment about to be poured out on Egypt in Isaiah 19:1. Identical words are used in connection to the Son of Man in the Olivet Discourse. An interesting question arises in conjunction with the phrase, "coming on the clouds." If "coming on the clouds" meant the Second Coming here, shouldn't the people be rejoicing? But they are not. Jesus, the Son of Man, is said to be coming on the clouds with power and great

The Abomination of Desolation

glory, and the people are in mourning. The people of Israel are mourning because the destruction of their Temple and holy city Jerusalem was *the sign* that the Son of Man was seated in heaven. The knee-jerk reaction of many to automatically kick any mention of the words "clouds," or "coming," to the end of time and space remains a mystery to me. Declaring that all so-called "de-creation language" points to the future, especially to a future Great Tribulation, makes for exciting reading, but it does not comport with Scripture. The apostle Peter was an eye-witness to the strange events that occurred just fifty days after Jesus' crucifixion, at Pentecost. That morning was so mind-boggling that onlookers were accusing its participants of being drunk! Peter assures the snide accusers, "These people are not drunk, as you suppose. It's only nine in the morning!" He then startles the gathered crowd by equating the Pentecost outpouring of the Holy Spirit with the fulfillment of the prophecy of Joel—de-creation language and all!

> No, *this is what was spoken by the prophet Joel*: *In the last days*, God says, I will pour out my Spirit on all people ... I will show wonders in the heavens above and signs on the earth below, blood and fire and billows of smoke. The sun will be turned to darkness and the moon to blood before the coming of the great and glorious day of the Lord. And everyone who calls on the name of the Lord will be saved.
> –Acts 2:16–21

Peter continues, "Jesus is exalted to the right hand of God, he has received from the Father the promised Holy Spirit and has poured out what you now see and hear ... Let all Israel be assured of this: God has made this Jesus, whom you crucified, both Lord and Messiah" (Acts 2:33, 36). The people were cut to the heart, and pleaded, "Brothers, what shall we do?" Peter replied, "Repent and be baptized, every one of you, in the name of Jesus Christ for the forgiveness of your sins. And you will receive the gift of the Holy

Spirit." Both Joel and Peter mention the cryptic "last days," and looking back, we know it wasn't the end of the world. No, but it was the end of the old way of doing things. It was the end of the Old Covenant, and nothing would ever be the same.

The LORD used the Roman Emperor Vespasian, and his son Titus, to bring about Israel's punishment for rejecting Jesus. Daniel's vision said the "people of the Prince" would come and destroy Jerusalem, and many of those who believed in Jesus bore witness to the armies of Rome coming in like a flood and swallowing up their beloved city. The Anointed One, Jesus, had burst onto the scene after "sixty-nine weeks," just as the angel Gabriel had told Daniel. He was put to death, "cut off" in the most excruciating fashion. This happened in the midst of the *seventieth* week, after just three-and-a-half years of ministry. Jesus had completed everything on God's "To-Do List" within the determined time constraint of the 70 weeks. He went out, not with a flailing gasp, but like autumn leaves, blazing in the light of glory. Knowing that he had finished the work his heavenly Father sent him to do, he mustered up his last ounce of strength and exhaled one final triumphant word, "*Tetelestai*!" One word was all he had left. We know that one word as three—"It is finished!"[63]

Nothing appeared triumphant in the weeks following the crucifixion. Jesus was gone. Eleven shook-up disciples seemed clueless as to "What's next?" Some had already returned to their prior professions. They did not experience what Mary did, up close and personal, in the garden after Jesus' resurrection. She got to see Jesus just before he ascended to the right hand of the Ancient of Days. Recall what Jesus said to Mary when she hugged him and wouldn't let go.[64] "*Do not hold on to me, for I have not yet ascended*

---

[63] John 19:30.

[64] He at first addresses her as "Woman." But when he speaks her name in Aramaic, "Miriam," everything changes.

to the Father. Go instead to my brothers and tell them, 'I am ascending to my Father and your Father, to my God and your God'" (John 20:17). This heavenly reunion is presented in Daniel chapter seven, immediately after the vision of the four wild beasts, representing the existing and subsequent world empires.[65] The scene suddenly changes to the throne room of God. There we are introduced to the Ancient of Days—the LORD Himself, and who should approach His throne but *one like a son of man, coming with the clouds* of heaven. Listen to what is declared next, for it is not what you will hear from the lips of those who are taught Futurism:

> *He was given authority, glory and sovereign power*; all nations and peoples of every language worshiped him. *His dominion is an everlasting dominion* that will not pass away, and his kingdom is one that will never be destroyed.
> –Daniel 7:14

Jesus had fulfilled his role as the Final Passover Lamb on the cross. Now, like the high priest who entered into the pattern of the Holy of Holies once a year at the Feast of Atonement, Jesus now enters into the real Holiest Place, offering his own blood once-for-all as the payment for sin, and he does this before his Father—the Ancient of Days. The wrath that is poured out on Jerusalem, one generation after Jesus' death, *is the sign* that the Son of Man is now seated at the right hand of the heavenly Father. Shortly after this, Jesus will appear to Thomas, offering to show him his nail-pierced hands; living proof that, just as the escape goat on the Day of Atonement, the people could see with their own eyes what had gone on in the Presence of the Ancient of Days. Now when you read Matthew 24:30, it might have new significance for you,

---

[65] The four wild beasts and their representative world empires are described in greater detail in Chapter 8.

> Then will appear *the sign of the Son of Man in heaven.* And then all the peoples of the earth will mourn when they see the Son of Man coming on the clouds of heaven, with power and great glory.

What I believe confuses people the most about the interpretation of apocalyptic literature is the projecting into the future of events that have already taken place. The next few highly figurative verses in the Olivet Discourse are mistakenly placed at the end of time and space. Jesus is telling his first-century disciples to heed the signs that he will be coming soon on the clouds of judgment. "Be prepared," he warns, "to flee Jerusalem when you get the chance."[66] One generation before judgment fell upon Jerusalem, Jesus stated,

> Truly I tell you, this generation will certainly not pass away until all these things have happened.
> –Matthew 24:34

How can one get around this and still call themselves a "literalist?" You can't. Futurists miss this incredible prophetic pronouncement of Jesus when they defer his kingdom and then project these events into the future. Others have missed it for other reasons. We turn to that now.

---

[66] Comparison could be made to the warning to Lot and his family prior to the judgment of Sodom and Gomorrah— "Don't look back!" Later, Jesus will liken his Second Coming to the days of Noah, when for those who are not "on board," it will be too late.

CHAPTER 8:

Jesus Was Not Wrong--or Lying!

Albert Schweitzer was best known as a great humanitarian for his life's work as a medical doctor in Africa. At age forty, he made the noble decision to "no longer speak or talk," but to *act* on behalf of poor natives who had no proper medical treatment. He was also influential in theology. Unfortunately, his writings were not orthodox Christian theology. His *Quest for the Historical Jesus* led him far astray from the biblical Jesus. Schweitzer believed Jesus: (1) brought about His own crucifixion; (2) did not undergo a resurrection; (3) had a "Messiah complex"; (4) thought he could bring about the end of the world by forcing His own death; and (5) was wrong about prophesying, "Before this generation passes, all these things shall occur." Why do you suppose Schweitzer believed that Jesus was wrong about the time of his coming? It appears his conclusion was based on a Futurist view that Jesus was speaking about the end of the world and not about his coming, in judgment, on that generation. When the generation after Jesus' death did not bring about the end of the world, Schweitzer concluded Jesus was wrong. I contend that it was Schweitzer, not Jesus, who was wrong. The same goes for Futurism pushing Jesus' warning into the distant future. Consistency requires one to believe Jesus meant what he said; making his words refer to the distant future necessitates jumping through too many hoops. Several of these "hermeneutical hoops" require too much of a leap.[67]

The easiest way to make sense of Jesus' words, "Before *this generation* passes away ..." is to determine what he meant by his "coming." He was not wrong if he was referring to coming (*erchomai*) in judgment within one generation. That does not preclude his Second Coming (*Parousia*) in the future, but it helps make sense of his words spoken to believers in the first century. Is there any precedent for interpreting "coming" in the sense of judgment? There is. Recall that Isaiah spoke of the Lord coming on the clouds of judgment against Egypt:

> See, *the Lord rides on a swift cloud and is coming* to Egypt. The idols of Egypt tremble before him, and the hearts of the Egyptians melt with fear.
> –Isaiah 19:1

What was the precedent for believing Messiah was going to come, in any fashion, as Daniel had prophesied? Expectancy was running high for the appearance of Israel's Messiah as a result of more than just Daniel's vision in Chapter 9. The prophet had received other visions during his time in Babylon. He had two visions concerning world empires that were spaced about fifty years apart. The first vision seems to be from the perception of man. Man sees world empires as precious metals. In the case of the first vision, those metals, in declining value, were gold, silver, bronze, and iron mixed with clay. The second vision depicts world empires as God sees them—as wild beasts. Those beasts are a lion, bear, leopard, and a composite beast of frightening countenance.

---

[67] The word "hermeneutics" derives from the Greek to suggest interpretation or explanation. Hermeneutics is connected to Hermes, herald of the gods, who was also known as the multifarious god of words, symbols, imagination, mischief, roads, thievery, merchants, athletics, travelers, even lies!

An outline is provided below, showing you the items contained in the visions as well as the empires they represented.[68]

Daniel 2	Daniel 7	Empire/Kingdom
Gold	Lion	Babylon (Daniel 2:38; 7:4)
Silver	Bear	Media-Persia (2:39; 7:5; 8:20)
Bronze	Leopard	Greece (2:39; 7:6; 8:5–8, 21)
Iron/Clay	Beast: A composite	Rome (2:40–45; 7:7,19f)

Stone cut without hands	[*Lamb; implied*]†	Kingdom of God (Matthew 28:18)

Italics were used in the center column for the Lamb because the text does not mention the lamb in print. Once we examine a few Scriptures, however, you will see how that vacant spot practically screams the Lamb's name—"Jesus!" The obvious place to start is John the Baptist, Jesus' cousin, who declared, "Look, *the Lamb* who takes away the sin of the world!" (John 1:29). Where did he get this from? I suggest he either deciphered it from the Book of Daniel, or, more likely, it was revealed to him by Jesus himself. It fits perfectly with the parallel vision of the precious metals and the Stone.

The Stone does not appear to be lustrous; there is nothing of beauty or majesty to attract us to it, nothing in its appearance that we

---

[68] Daniel 7 and 8 should be read together as other animals are introduced (a ram with two horns, a he-goat with a notable horn, a rough goat) to explain in greater detail the history of the bear and leopard kingdoms.

should desire it (cf. Isaiah 53:2). But this "Stone" is a supernatural stone, "cut without hands," that is empowered to strike down and pulverize the statue made of more impressive metals. Similarly, the Lamb is the least of any of these mighty animals, and yet, it devours these wild beasts as easily as Moses' staff-turned-serpent devoured the serpent of Pharaoh's magicians.[69] Christ established his everlasting kingdom, and there will never be another world empire again. Satan will, according to Revelation 20, make one final, last ditch attempt at defying God, but rather than an individual Antichrist controlling all things, it envisions Satan, after being "bound for 1,000 years," being unleashed for a short season in order to gather all the forces of evil against the Church. That does not exclude the possibility of wealthy oligarchs consolidating their money, power, and influence behind one world leader. I would just caution against taking such a dogmatic stance about a seven-year tribulation Antichrist that you might miss other important signs of the times.

Keep in mind, the Lord Jesus Christ has already won the victory. The resurrection of Christ was equivalent to the mating net in a game of chess; the game is already over. The progression of history is merely finishing out the remaining moves. Checkmate, the final "mopping up" operation, will occur at the Second Coming when the saints (starting with the dead in Christ) rise up to meet Jesus and accompany him for the Final Judgment and the restoration in the new heavens and new earth.

Judgment upon Israel

Why would Christ come in judgment against Israel you might ask? Read Luke 19:41–44,

---

[69] Exodus 7:8–12. Serpent/Dragon was a symbol of satanically inspired pagan culture. Three kinds of "dragons" are spoken of in Scripture: Tannin, Leviathan, and the "proud one" Rahab. See Isaiah 27:1; Psalm 87:4; 89:10; 91:12–13; 104:26; Job 26:12–13. From Chilton, *Days of Vengeance*, 304.

> As he approached Jerusalem and saw the city, he wept over it and said, If you, even you, had only known on this day what would bring you peace—but now it is hidden from your eyes. The days will come upon you when your enemies will build an embankment against you and encircle you and hem you in on every side. They will dash you to the ground, you and the children within your walls. They will not leave one stone on another, *because you did not recognize the time of God's coming to you.*

In a similar vein:

> You snakes! You brood of vipers! How will you escape being condemned to hell? Truly I tell you, all this will come *on this generation.* Jerusalem, Jerusalem, you who kill the prophets and stone those sent to you, how often I have longed to gather your children together, as a hen gathers her chicks under her wings, and you were not willing. *Look, your house is left to you desolate ...* –Matthew 23:33, 36–38

Jesus had previously warned Israel of the consequences of repeatedly disobeying God in the Parable of the Vineyard Owner. This colorful story relates what would happen to the wicked tenants who had mistreated and killed everyone the vineyard owner had sent. The owner finally sent his son, figuring they would at least respect him. But they would kill him as well, sealing their doom. Israel represented the wicked tenants in the parable, as it was they who repeatedly mistreated the prophets that God, the vineyard owner, had sent. "*We have no king but Caesar!*" they cried, shortly before having God's son Jesus hauled off and hoisted on a cross (John 19:15). How could a God of justice *not* punish Israel for rejecting His own Son? In this modern era of Universalism, "A loving God would never do that; everyone is welcome into His kingdom," the thought of a just God who metes out punishment is a hard pill to swallow. But that is the God of the Bible—holiness demands justice. "His blood be on us and on our children!" they shouted at Pilate (Matthew 27:25 KJV). The irony of that prophetic statement is too sad to ponder. It leads me to ask, "How could Israel miss Jesus as the Messiah?" There are so many wonderful pictures of Messiah in the Old Testament; there is just no excuse for them rejecting the one who so perfectly mirrored what those images were mere reflections of. Let's take a look at them now.

CHAPTER 9:

Pictures of Jesus in the Old Testament

The Old Testament provides us with numerous examples of foreshadowing the Messiah. These word pictures remind us of the importance of prophetic literature. Here is a list of just some of those major prophetic pictures and themes:

> Tree of Life
> River of Life
> Theme of "Head-crushing"
> Stone/Rock
> Light of the World
> Living Water
> Resurrection
> The Breath of Life
> Root/Shoot/Stem of Jesse
> Righteous Branch

The Tree of Life

The Tree of Life first appears in the Garden of Eden. It was off limits, as was the Tree of the Knowledge of Good and Evil. Once Adam and Eve had eaten of the forbidden tree, God put them out of the Garden of Eden, lest they also eat of the Tree of Life and become His eternal enemies. This Tree of Life was later stylized in the form of a seven-branched golden lampstand. This lampstand, or menorah, was placed within the Holy Place of the Tabernacle, and later, the

Temple. Jesus, as the true Tree of Life, is seen by the apostle John, in a vision, standing in the midst of seven golden lampstands as the antitype of the stylized Tree of Life.

> And when I turned I saw seven golden lampstands, and among the lampstands was someone like a son of man.
> –Revelation 1:13

River of Life

The Garden of Eden had a river running through it, splitting into four heads, flowing to the four corners of the earth. Ezekiel 47 depicts a stream of water flowing eastward from God's Temple. This stream, interestingly, got deeper and wider the farther one got from the Temple to the point it became a river that no one could cross. This river flowed in every direction, providing life-giving water everywhere it went. Even the Dead Sea is depicted as coming back to life! The land surrounding the river would be fertile, as trees lined the banks. The kingdom of God would grow in a similar fashion to this river. Yet, not every area would be converted to good land. "But the swamps and marshes will not become fresh; they will be left for salt" (47:11). The same river shows up again in the very last chapter of the Bible—

> Then the angel showed me the river of the water of life, as clear as crystal, flowing from the throne of God and of the Lamb down the middle of the great street of the city. On each side of the river stood the tree of life, bearing twelve crops of fruit, yielding its fruit every month. And the leaves of the tree are for the healing of the nations.
> –Revelation 22:1–2

The river is a powerful metaphor for the change that takes place within a Believer when the Holy Spirit is allowed to flow. The kingdom of God leads to change for the better. Jesus used the example of a mustard seed to illustrate how his kingdom would have a small beginning but grow like a mighty oak in which the birds would nest. He bolstered this concept with another illustration, that of how a tiny lump of yeast (leaven) transforms the entire loaf of bread. The yeast not only causes the loaf to expand (literally), it also transforms the room it is in, its aroma filling the entire house (Matthew 13:31–33).

Theme of "Head-crushing"

In hindsight, we can see a hint of the head-crushing theme very early on in Genesis 3:15. Genesis 3:15 is the fountainhead of all prophecy. The serpent would bruise the seed of the woman, but her descendant would crush the serpent's head. This theme of "head-crushing" is sprinkled throughout Scripture: (1) young David slings a stone to the forehead of Goliath; (2) Sisera, the commander of one of Israel's great enemies, had his head crushed by a woman, Jael, when she put a tent peg through his temple as he slept (Judges 4:21; 5); (3) Gideon's wicked son Abimelech had his skull crushed by a millstone cast by a woman in a tower (Judges 9:53); (4) the Psalmist declares, "Surely God will crush the heads of his enemies" (Psalm 68:21). God has evil by the head and toe (or tail, in the case of the serpent), as seen in Daniel 2 where the "Stone cut without hands" took down the statue of precious metals by striking it in the feet. Jesus seems to have received inspiration from this last theme from Daniel for his role as God's "Stone." His parables of the mustard seed and the leaven parallel the growth of that "Stone" in Daniel 2. They point us back to the Fall and direct us forward to Golgotha, where God planted His "Stone" on the forehead of the place called "The Skull" (John 19:17).†

One way to crush a serpent's head is with the heel of your foot; another way is with a rock ...

The Stone/Rock

One of the most well-known stories of the Bible is that of Moses being commanded by God to strike a rock in order to produce water for the people of Israel in the wilderness. He obeyed God, and the people were spared. Nearly forty years later, Moses was commanded to "speak to the rock" and bring forth water. In this instance, however, Moses, fed up with all of the grumbling, struck the rock in anger, saying, "Listen, you rebels!" "Must we bring you water out of this rock?"[70] As a result of his disobedience, Moses was denied leading the people of Israel into the Promised Land. That form of punishment from God seems harsh; Moses certainly had the right to be angry with the people. Why do you suppose the LORD was so harsh in this case? It was because, in striking the rock a second time, Moses was shattering a beautiful picture of Christ, who was to be smitten once, and only once, for sin.[71] It was no surprise to God that Israel would be stubborn and would reject His loving provision. The Book of Deuteronomy, which means "Second Law," refers to God as the Rock; a faithful God who does no wrong and who is upright and just (32:3–4). But hear what the LORD has to say to Israel:

> They are corrupt and not his children; to their shame they are a warped and crooked generation ... You deserted the Rock, who fathered you; you forgot the God who gave you birth ... I will hide my face from them, he said, and see what their end will be; for they are a perverse generation, children who are unfaithful... They made me jealous by what is no god and angered me with their worthless idols. I will make them envious by those who are not a people; I

---

[70] See Exodus 17 and Numbers 20 for the account of these two events.
[71] Malcolm Smith, *Exodus Volume I*, tape series, (San Antonio: Malcolm Smith Ministries), tape X.

will make them angry by a nation that has no understanding.
—Deuteronomy 32:5,18–21

Messiah would be a "stone that causes Israel to stumble and a rock that makes them fall," says the prophet Isaiah (8:14). Jesus makes the same point when he combines the stone/rock images from Isaiah, Daniel, and the Psalms in his Parable of the Vineyard Owner in Matthew 21:33–46:[72]

> Therefore, I tell you that the kingdom of God will be taken away from you and given to a people who will produce its fruit. *Anyone who falls on this stone will be broken* to pieces; anyone on whom it falls will be *crushed.*

This parable ends with the telling statement, "When the chief priests and the Pharisees heard Jesus' parables, *they knew he was talking about them.*" Ouch!

Nearly every Christian is familiar with the Psalmist's reference to the Messiah in the phrase, "The stone the builders rejected has become the cornerstone" (Psalm 118:22). But did you know, long before Jesus ever set foot in Galilee, a real-life builder had already rejected her? Yes. His name was Hiram, king of Tyre. King Solomon had gifted twenty cities within Galilee to Hiram for supplying him with all the cedar and juniper and gold he wanted for building the temple. Upon inspection, however, Galilee did not "cut it." Hiram rejected the gift, saying, "You can keep your twenty cities." He even gave these cities a name—Kabul, meaning "Good for nothing," or "Refuse" (1 Kings 9:10–13). Galilee may have been "good for nothing" in the eyes of King Hiram and derided by many living in the first century—"Can anything good come out of

---

[72] Psalm 118:22, Isaiah 8:14; 28:16, and Daniel 2:34–35. I can't imagine it went over well when said, "Have you never read in the Scriptures?" to the religious "scholars" of the day (Matthew 21:42)!

Galilee?"; "Are you also from Galilee?"[73] But God had other plans. The area of Galilee was first to fall into Babylonian captivity. That is the bad news. The good news is, according to Isaiah 9:1–2, Galilee would also be the first to see the light of the coming Messiah—"The people that walked in darkness have seen a great light."

Despite all the trash-talk about Galilee, she was the first to hear the Gospel of Jesus Christ.

> Now when Jesus heard that John had been put in prison, He departed *to Galilee.* And leaving Nazareth, He came and dwelt in Capernaum, which is by the sea, in the regions of Zebulun and Naphtali, that it might be fulfilled which was spoken by Isaiah the prophet*,* saying: The land of Zebulun and the land of Naphtali, by the way of the sea, beyond the Jordan, *Galilee of the Gentiles: The people who sat in darkness have seen a great light,* and upon those who sat in the region and shadow of death, *light has dawned.*
>
> —Matthew 4:12–16

That leads us to the next picture of Christ—

Light of the World

The Jews, in the form of the Golden Candlestick placed in the Holy Place of the Temple, held a brilliant picture of the transforming character that would be contained in the Messiah. The menorah, as it is called, not only represented the Tree of Life, it also looked forward to the One who would be the Light of the world. Jesus boldly proclaimed, "I am the Light of the world" in John

---

[73] John 1:46 and John 7:52.

8:12.[74] David loved to sing out his praises to God—"You, Lord, are my lamp; the Lord turns my darkness into light" (2 Samuel 22:29). One of the best-loved verses in all of the Bible is, "Your word is a lamp unto my feet, and a light unto my path" (Psalm 119:105). Light is considered a good thing by most, but not by cockroaches—or sinners.

John the Baptist was sent to bear witness that Jesus is the Light, the true Light that gives light to every man coming into the world (John 1:6–9). Jesus was/is the "light in the darkness." Though this light was first shown in Galilee, it was not just for the Jews. Time and time again, the Old Testament prophets foretold the fulfillment of the original promise made to Abram, "Through you, *all* the nations of the world will be blessed" (Genesis 12:3). Hear the words of Isaiah:

> Arise, shine, for your light has come, and the glory of the Lord rises upon you. See, darkness covers the earth and thick darkness is over the peoples, but the Lord rises upon you and his glory appears over you. Nations will come to your light, and kings to the brightness of your dawn.
> –Isaiah 60:1–3

Living Water

Isaiah 12:2–3 proclaims,

> Surely God is my salvation; I will trust and not be afraid. The LORD, the LORD himself, is my strength

---

[74] These "I am" declarations in the book of John are called the "*Ego eimi*" statements of Christ. They include the Bread of Life (6:35, 41, 48, 51); Light of the World (8:12); Door (10:2, 7, 9); Good Shepherd (10:11, 14); Resurrection and the Life (11:25); Way, Truth, Life (14:6); and True Vine (15:1, 5). These seven "*ego eimi*" metaphors reflect the seven Redeemer names of God of the Old Testament.

and my defense; he has become my salvation. With
joy you will *draw water from the wells of salvation.*

Those familiar with Scripture will recall the conversation in John 4 between Jesus and the Samaritan woman at Jacob's well where he tells her, "If you knew the gift of God and who it is that asks you for a drink, you would have asked him and he would have given you living water. Everyone who drinks this water will be thirsty again, but whoever drinks the water I give them will never thirst. Indeed, the water I give them will become in them a spring of water welling up to eternal life" (4:10–13).

Due to the strict literal stance of Futurism, many miss the symbolic meaning of much of Scripture. The "living waters" in these passages have nothing to do with literal water. Jesus was not talking about some kind of special, "living water" in John 7:27–38 when he stood up on the last and greatest day of the Feast of Tabernacles and said in a loud voice, "Let anyone who is thirsty come to me and drink.[75] Whoever believes in me, as Scripture has said, *rivers of living water will flow from within them.*" If you have any doubts, the very next verse clarifies exactly what Jesus meant:

> By this *he meant the Spirit*, whom those who believed in him were later to receive. Up to that time the Spirit had not been given, since Jesus had not yet been glorified.

Old Testament "Resurrections"

The idea of the miracle of resurrection was planted in the minds of the Israelites long before they became a nation. Look at the trouble Sarah and Rebekah had at child-bearing. Sarah was reproductively a "dead stick" when God promised she and Abram they would have a

---

[75] This last, eighth day added on to Tabernacles is known as *Shemini Atzeret*, the *eighth* [day] of assembly. No water was poured out on this day, as the first and eighth days of Tabernacles were considered sabbaths (Leviticus 23:36, 39).

child of their own. Zachariah and Elisabeth were in the same predicament before John the Baptist was miraculously brought forth. Speaking of "dead sticks," God commanded Moses to lay the wooden tribal staffs before the LORD, in front of the ark of the covenant, so that He could demonstrate who was in charge. In the morning, one "dead stick" had come back to life. It was Aaron's staff that had "resurrected;" not only had it sprouted, it had budded, blossomed, and produced almonds as well (Numbers 17:1–9).

The promised child Isaac was "dead" in the eyes of his father Abraham for three days after God told Abraham to offer his son up as a sacrifice on Mt. Moriah, the same site that God would offer up His own son Jesus—the site of the future temple in Jerusalem (see 2 Chronicles 3:1). Hebrews 11:19 tells us, "Abraham reasoned that God could even raise the dead," and so in a manner of speaking, he did receive Isaac back from death (Hebrews 11:19). He clung to this belief for the entire three-day journey, right up to the moment an angel of the LORD stayed his hand and spared Isaac's life by means of a substitute sacrifice (Genesis 22:1–14).

God also provided for a grieving Shunammite woman. She and her elderly husband were given a miracle child much like Abraham and Sarah, but then her son died. God brought Elisha along to breathe life back into the child (2 Kings 4). It was right next door to Shunem, in Nain, that Jesus would also raise a widow's only son back to life with the words, "Young man, I say to you, arise!" (Luke 7:11–16).

In 2 Samuel 7:12, the LORD tells King David, "I will *raise up* your offspring to succeed you, your own flesh and blood, and I will establish his kingdom." The *Septuagint* (*LXX*), the Greek version of the Old Testament, uses an interesting word to translate the Hebrew "set up," or "raise up," in this verse. It uses *"resurrect"* (*anastēso*), suggesting that this ultimate "Son of David," whose kingdom would be everlasting, would be known for being raised from the dead. Ding! Ding! Ding! If you made the connection to Jesus, you win the prize.

The Breath of Life

Even before God created life, His *Spirit* is said to have "hovered over" the waters of the chaotic early stages of the Universe. The word "spirit" (*ruach* in Hebrew, *pneuma* in Greek) is the same word used for *breath, wind, air.* God "breathed" His Spirit of life into the newly- formed Adam in Genesis 2, much like Elisha breathed life back into the dead son of the Shunammite woman. The well-known story of the "dry bones," a picture of Israel in exile, dried up and all out of hope, depicts a valley of lifeless corpses brought back to life after God breathed His Spirit into them; a metaphor for the New Life that Israel will be granted when Jesus is resurrected.

> These bones are the people of Israel. They say, Our bones are dried up and our hope is gone; we are cut off ... *I am going to open your graves* ... You, my people, will know that I am the Lord, when I open your graves and bring you up from them. *I will put my Spirit in you and you will live*, and I will settle you in your own land. Then you will know that I the Lord have spoken.
>
> —Ezekiel 37:11f

Futurists tend to lock onto the phrase "I will settle you in your own land" to argue that this is referring to Jews settling into modern-day Israel. But Abraham was not longing for a piece of real estate on the Mediterranean Sea, and neither should we. Hebrews 11 tells us that Abraham looked for a city whose architect and builder is God—a heavenly country. God is not interested in geography. He is interested in hearts that are open to Him. How do we know the "Dry Bones" metaphor was talking about the spiritual rebirth of Israel?

Where else in Scripture does it speak of "graves being opened"? When Jesus was resurrected—

> And when Jesus had cried out again in a loud voice, he gave up his spirit. At that moment the curtain of the temple was torn in two from top to bottom ... *The bodies of many holy people who had died were raised to life. They came out of the tombs after Jesus' resurrection* and went into the holy city and appeared to many people.
> —Matthew 27:50–53

Not even a hardened Roman centurion could deny what his eyes were seeing. His testimony to the day's events is recorded for posterity, "Surely he was the Son of God!" (Matthew 27:54). It is this message that we need to share with Jews living today: "Jesus is the Son of God." Jesus breathed the Holy Spirit into his disciples after his resurrection;[76] the Jews can receive this same infusion of the Holy Spirit if they will only accept Jesus as the one historical figure who fulfills every aspect of the Old Testament prophets— more than three hundred! Most Jews flat-out refuse to read the New Testament. Perhaps they need to be reminded that reading a book about Hitler does not make one a Nazi. No one is going to force them to believe; that is between them and God.

Root/Stump of Jesse

We get the first hint that the Messiah would not come riding in on a white stallion, like normal kings might do, in the anointing of the young David. Reminiscent of the stepsisters in the fairy tale Cinderella, the slipper didn't fit the first seven sons of Jesse. David was but a "little shoot," out tending the sheep, probably not even

---

[76] John 20:22.

considered a legitimate son by his own brothers.[77] It was through the lineage of David, however, that the ultimate king of Israel, Messiah, would come. Isaiah refers to the coming Messiah in this fashion:

> A *shoot will come up from the stump* of Jesse; *from his roots a Branch* will bear fruit. The Spirit of the LORD will rest on him ... He will not judge by what he sees with his eyes, or decide by what he hears with his ears; but with righteousness he will judge ...
> —Isaiah 11:1–4

Just as the prophet Samuel was directed not to judge the sons of Jesse with his eyes, it is said that God's Anointed would judge in righteousness, looking at the heart (1 Samuel 16:7; Isaiah 11:3). Closely connected to the picture of the "Shoot" is its outgrowth—the Branch.

The Righteous Branch

The Jews were also told of a "Branch" that would come in the form of their Messiah, ushering in righteousness. The Nazarene denomination derives its name from the "Branch" *(netzer)*. In fact, one of the covenant names of God is directly connected with this branch. It is found in Jeremiah 23:5–6. It is mind-boggling how the people of Israel missed it.

> The days are coming, declares the Lord, when I will raise up for David *a righteous Branch*, a King who will reign wisely and do what is just and right in the land. In his days Judah will be saved and Israel will live in safety. This is the name by which he will be called: *The Lord Our Righteousness.*

---

[77] The Talmud has it that David's brothers treated him with contempt, considering him to be illegitimate. Psalm 51:5 and 69:4, 8 give some credence to this idea. For more on this, research Nitzevet.

Again, how could the Jews miss Jesus as their Messiah? Only if their concept of who he is was incorrect. Jesus can even be seen in Jacob, the first Israelite. Jacob rolled away a stone and brought forth "living water" for the flock in Genesis 29:3.† He was a forerunner of Christ, who, by means of a stone being rolled away, brought forth life to all who believe. Jesus became the first Israelite of the New Covenant (Mark 16:3–4). But judgment is never God's final word to Israel; He wants nothing more than to have them back in the fold, grafted back into His "Olive Tree" (Romans 11). For that to happen, some "Spiritual Horticulture" must take place. Get your pruning shears ready, and let's dig in.

CHAPTER 10:

Of Shepherds, Vines, and Olive Trees

The True Vine

> I am the true vine, and my Father is the gardener. I am the vine; you are the branches. If you remain in me and I in you, you will bear much fruit; apart from me you can do nothing.
>
> —John 15:1, 5

What was Jesus implying? If there is a True Vine, then there are also false vines. Jesus connects the two concepts of vine and branch when he states, "I am the vine, and you are the branches." Israel as a vine was not a new concept; there are numerous times where she is referred to as a vine. Problem is, the vine as applied to Israel in the Old Testament is always negative. In Isaiah 5, she is the vineyard, carefully and lovingly planted by God, but which only produced "bad grapes." In Ezekiel 15 and 17, Israel is spoken of as a vine that is practically useless.

> Therefore, thus says the Lord God: Like the wood of the vine among the trees of the forest, which I have *given to the fire for fuel, so I will give up the inhabitants of Jerusalem*; and I will set My face against them. They will go out from one fire, but

> another fire shall devour them. Then you shall know that I am the Lord, when I set My face against them.
> –Ezekiel 15:6, 7

> Say to them, This is what the Sovereign Lord says: Will it thrive? Will it not be uprooted and stripped of its fruit so that it withers? All its new growth will wither. It will not take a strong arm or many people to pull it up by the roots.
> –Ezekiel 17:9

You can't build with a vine. About the only thing it is good for is keeping a fire going, hence Israel is likened to two cities along the Dead Sea that were famously destroyed when God poured out His wrath in the form of fire and brimstone. The Dead Sea remains "dead" to this day—

> Their vine comes from the vine of Sodom and from the fields of Gomorrah. Their grapes are filled with poison, and their clusters with bitterness.
> –Deuteronomy 32:32

Jeremiah 2:21 speaks of God planting Israel as a noble vine, a seed of highest quality, then asks the rhetorical question, "How then have you turned before Me into a *degenerate plant; an alien vine?*"

The Olive Tree

The Olive Tree is another metaphor used to represent Israel in the Bible. The apostle Paul describes how Israel is like branches broken off an olive tree due to her unbelief in Jesus as the Messiah. It was due to the Jews' unbelief, he says, that the Gentiles were grafted into this olive tree. Paul longs for his fellow countrymen to turn from their current state of unbelief, to repent and be grafted into the tree again. He concludes his illustration by stating,

> Israel has experienced a hardening in part until the full number of the Gentiles has come in, and *in this way all Israel will be saved.*
>
> –Romans 11:25–26

Israel will not get into God's kingdom simply for being Jewish. Paul, a Jew himself, emphasizes this point when he states, "Not all who are descended from Israel are Israel. Nor because they are his descendants are they all Abraham's children" (Romans 9:6–7). This revelation was made known to Paul via his conversion. He had to be blinded in order to see. Acts 9 is the account of Paul, still known as Saul, setting out for Damascus to persecute Christians. When he was suddenly blinded, a voice said to him, "Saul, Saul, why do you persecute me?" Saul obviously realized he was experiencing something supernatural, as he asked, "Who are you, Lord?" "I am Jesus, whom you are persecuting ..." (Acts 9:4–5). In an instant, Saul's life was transformed. Three days later, his eyes were opened, literally and figuratively, and he immediately began preaching salvation through the Lord Jesus Christ.

Why was this so important? It is important because then, as now, the majority of the Jews did not believe Jesus was the Messiah. Paul, like his predecessor Jesus, was also rejected, which led to Paul turning to the Gentiles and proclaiming the "Good News" of the Gospel to them.

The Good Shepherd

Just as there were "false vines," there were "false Shepherds." In John 10:10, Jesus declares, "I am the Good Shepherd." Once again, this sets him up in contrast to the false shepherds that have been neglecting the flock of Israel. Israel was *supposed* to be a Shepherd to all nations (fulfilling the promise to father Abraham), but they failed. Hear these words from the prophet Ezekiel:

> Son of man, prophesy against the shepherds of Israel ... Woe to you shepherds of Israel who only take care of yourselves ... You have not brought back the strays or searched for the lost ... they were scattered because there was no shepherd ... and no one searched or looked for them ... Therefore, you shepherds, hear the word of the Lord ... I am against the shepherds and will hold them accountable ... This is what the Sovereign Lord says: I myself will search for my sheep and look after them.
> —Ezekiel 34:2–11

Later in the same chapter, Ezekiel states something quite amazing, considering King David was long gone by this point,

> *I will place over them one shepherd, my servant David*, and he will tend them; he will tend them and be their shepherd. I the Lord will be their God, and my servant David will be prince among them.
> —Ezekiel 34:23–24

Just who do Jews think Ezekiel is talking about? Jesus certainly thought that he had been sent by God the Father for this very purpose. He, like Paul, longs for his beloved Israel to think that too. One parable in the New Testament that is a favorite among many Christians is that of the shepherd who leaves the ninety-nine sheep in order to go after the one lost lamb. Jesus tells this parable right alongside those of the "Lost Coin" and the "Prodigal Son." Jesus cleverly delegates the role of the prodigal son to himself, as that is how the Pharisees saw him. The Pharisees are assigned the role of the elder brother. The elder brother is the one role you do not want to play in this parable. The elder brother's snide remark, "This *son of yours*" is countered by the loving father's reply, "This *brother of yours*" (Luke 15:30, 32).

Central in the Parable of the Lost Son is the father. In the parable, the father is willing to disgrace himself if it means shielding his sons from shame or embarrassment. He did the unthinkable for a first-century Middle Eastern man when he hitched up his tunic and ran to his younger son before the citizens of the village could permanently banish the profligate young man from his family, his faith, and his community.[78] In an emotional reunion, the father made it clear that there would be no banishing done on that day. Despite what his son had done, he would not be rejected. The father took upon himself the full shame that should have fallen upon his son and invited all to a feast to welcome his son back home. At the feast, the father suffers the additional humiliation of having to leave his invited guests in order to go outside and deal with his ungrateful older son. The love and grace of the father in this parable mimics that of our heavenly Father. God bore the punishment due us when Jesus willingly endured the pain and shame of the cross on our behalf.

God longs to lavish everything on us. That is what the Good Shepherd does. Peter's restoration after denying knowing Jesus three times at his crucifixion entailed being told, three times, "Feed my lambs ... Shepherd my sheep ... Tend my sheep" (John 21:15–17). Jesus appears to be giving a nod to Zechariah 11, which not only mentions "feeding the flock" three times, but it also contains the verse, "So they weighed for my price thirty pieces of silver," the price Judas received for betraying Jesus (Zechariah 11:4,7,12; Matthew 26:15). Judas met a horrific end. Peter, meanwhile, was rewarded. His earlier confession of faith, "You are the Messiah, the Son of the living God," became the "rock" upon which the early Church was built, just as Jesus had promised (Mathew 16:16–18).

---

[78] The Jewish ritual known as *kezazah* entailed breaking a large clay pot in front of the offending individual and yelling, "You are now cut off from your people!" From a sermon by Pastor Jack Hilligoss of High Point Church of God in Lake Wales, FL on 27 FEB 2022

If you are Christian reading this, then it is highly likely that you are *not* Jewish. Think about it. We are only part of the body of Christ because Paul, a Jew, turned to the Gentiles, and he only turned to the Gentiles *after* the Jews turned on him.

> As Paul and Barnabas were leaving the synagogue, the people invited them to speak further about these things on the next Sabbath ... When the Jews saw the crowds, they were filled with jealousy. They began to contradict what Paul was saying and heaped abuse on him. Then Paul and Barnabas answered them boldly: We had to speak the word of God to you first. *Since you reject it* and do not consider yourselves worthy of eternal life, *we now turn to the Gentiles.*
> —Acts 13:42–45

Paul then takes on this mission as the fulfillment of Isaiah 49:6,

> I will also make you a light for the Gentiles that my salvation may reach to the ends of the earth.

Believers in Christ are united into one body through the blood of Jesus Christ. Unity in the Body of Christ was a message that Paul was passionate about. He drove that message home repeatedly:

> *There is neither Jew nor Gentile*, neither slave nor free, nor is there male and female, for *you are all one in Christ Jesus.*
> —Galatians 3:28

> This mystery is that through the gospel *the Gentiles are heirs together with Israel, members together of one body*, and sharers together in the promise in Christ Jesus.
> —Ephesians 3:6

> Put on the new self, which is being renewed in knowledge in the image of its Creator. Here there is

> no Gentile or Jew, circumcised or uncircumcised ...
> but Christ is all, and is in all.
> —Colossians 3:10–11

For Paul, Christ united all mankind into one "new man." This meant doing away with physical differences such as genealogical bloodlines or circumcision. In Romans 9:6–7 he states,

> For *not all who are descended from Israel are Israel.* Nor because they are his descendants are they all Abraham's children. On the contrary, It is through Isaac that your offspring will be reckoned.

Millions of Jews have returned to the small strip of land on the Mediterranean Sea now known as the nation of Israel. On May 14, 1948, Israel reclaimed its independence for the first time since 586 B.C. But changing your geography does not make you a Jew any more than climbing an apple tree makes you an apple. As we saw earlier with the relationship of Israel to the olive tree, being a true Israelite entails more than having Jewish blood flowing through one's veins. That being the case, just who is a true Israelite and how does one become part of that unique family? Let's take a look.

CHAPTER 11:

Circumcision of the Heart

In the Old Testament, for a man to be considered "in covenant with God" meant circumcision. Why in the world would God choose circumcision to be the sign of this covenant relationship? It is my belief that God chose this particular "marker" because of the choice that Adam made in the Garden of Eden. Rather than he and Eve, as one, putting God first, it seems Adam chose Eve, or more specifically, sex with Eve, over God. He opted for instant gratification rather than obedience to his Maker. That would explain why God chose to "punish" that particular male organ. It also helps make sense of the letter to Ephesus in chapter two of Revelation, where it warns its citizens against having their "lampstand" removed from its place.

> Yet I hold this against you: *You have forsaken your first love* ... If you do not repent, I will come to you and remove your lampstand from its place. Whoever has ears, let them hear what the Spirit says to the churches ... To the one who is victorious, I will give the right to *eat from the tree of life, which is in the paradise of God.*
>
> —Revelation 2:4–7

Adam and Eve were physically removed from the Garden because Adam had "left his first love"—God. Those of Ephesus would likewise be "put out of the garden," so to speak, if they did not return to Christ, their first love. But physical circumcision was never the point. God's intention was that man's heart would be turned to Him.

[Margin note: not to "punish" - but that they would be "fruitful" and "multiply".]

God's "Second Law" (Deuteronomy means "Second Law") has a different form of circumcision in mind—"The Lord your God will circumcise your hearts" (Deuteronomy 30:6; 10:15–16). A new "mark" was needed to signify the believer's covenant relationship with God in the New Covenant. That sign is baptism.

> In him you were also circumcised with a circumcision not performed by human hands. Your whole self ruled by the flesh was put off when you were *circumcised by Christ, having been buried with him in baptism*, in which you were also raised with him through your faith in the working of God, who raised him from the dead. For he has rescued us from the dominion of darkness and *brought us into the kingdom* of the Son he loves.
> —Colossians 2:11–13

In the outward act of baptism, the believer is indicating, "I am dead to sin, and I am raised up justified by means of the shed blood of Jesus Christ." "God raised us up with Christ and seated us with him in the heavenly realms in Christ Jesus," according to Paul in Ephesians 2:4–6. For those who are "born-again" (John 3), a "first resurrection" has occurred. There is no fear of what Scripture refers to as the "second death," the destiny awaiting those who have no part in the kingdom of God. Believers can rejoice in the fact that they reign with Christ, whether during their lifetime or in Paradise awaiting the Final Resurrection. "So we make it our goal," says Paul, "Whether we are at home in the body or away from it. For we must all appear before the judgment seat of Christ, so that each of us may receive what is due us for the things done while in the body, whether good or bad" (2 Corinthians 5:9–10). This is the separation of the "sheep" from the "goats" (Matthew 25:31–33). For the ungodly, this final judgment will be a time of great fear, but for the Christian, it will be like standing on the podium of an Olympic Award Ceremony.[79]

If the apostle Paul could say in the first century that God has brought us into the kingdom, then how can we not oppose any teaching that says Jesus' kingdom was rejected and his kingdom still awaits Christ's Return? In saying that, one is agreeing with the Pharisees! Read the account in John 3, of Jesus' conversation with Nicodemus (under the cover of darkness), about being "born-again." "You are '*The Teacher in Israel*,'" Jesus asks, "And you don't know these things?" Nicodemus struggled with taking words literally just as people do today. He did not grasp the concept of being "born again" at the time. He appears to have come to an understanding of the concept during the course of Jesus' ministry, however, as John 19:39 records how he and Joseph of Arimathea came to Pilate, at high risk to themselves, to procure the body of Christ.

We are now "one new man" in Christ, the middle wall of partition between Jew and Gentile has been torn down (Ephesians 2:11–22). It truly was a "new thing" for the Jews of the first century, and they had a hard time believing it. Paul had to be blinded in order to see it. Peter had to be shown a vision and told to eat unclean animals! This was unthinkable to a Jew. Yet, the vision was repeated three times, and a voice told him, "Do not call anything impure that God has made clean." The two primary witnesses of the early Church, Peter and Paul, had to have this revealed to them by God in back-to-back chapters—Acts 9 and 10. Now that God revealed this unifying act to them and had them record it in His Holy Word, are we now going to throw it all away? God forbid! Unity in Christ is one of the main themes of the New Covenant:

---

[79] The word for "judgment seat" or "tribunal of Christ" is *bēmatos (βήματος του χριστου)*.

> But now in Christ Jesus you who once were far away have been brought near by the blood of Christ. For he himself is our peace, who *has made the two groups one and has destroyed the barrier, the dividing wall of hostility*.
> –Ephesians 2:13–14

Sadly, the most popular current End-Times interpretation puts the wall back up! How so? Futurists are looking for a new Jewish temple to be rebuilt on the site that has remained vacant for nearly two thousand years. Perhaps there is a reason that the site has remained desolate. Technically, it is not empty; a Muslim mosque has occupied that site for hundreds of years now. But there is an even greater problem for the Futurist—Scripture. Try this experiment. Those of you who are teachers, ask your class to fill in the blank: "Your body is the _____ of the Holy Spirit." 99% of them will say "temple." Why do they answer that way? Because they have either read it or heard it many times:

> Don't you know that *you yourselves are God's temple* and that God's Spirit dwells in your midst?
> –1 Corinthians 3:16; see also 6:19

> In him the whole building is joined together and rises to become a holy temple in the Lord. And in him *you too are being built together to become a dwelling in which God lives by his Spirit*.
> –Ephesians 2:21–22

> What agreement is there between the temple of God and idols? *For we are the temple of the living God.*
> –2 Corinthians 6:16

> As you come to him, the living Stone—rejected by humans but chosen by God and precious to him—*you also, like living stones, are being built into a spiritual*

> *house* to be a holy priesthood, offering spiritual sacrifices acceptable to God through Jesus Christ.
> —1 Peter 2:4–5

Just as circumcision of the flesh was not God's primary intent, neither was a physical temple. Surely you recall Jesus' words, "[You all] Destroy this temple, and I will raise it up in three days" (John 2:19). This was one of the false accusations brought against him in the illegal "trial" leading up to his crucifixion, as they said, "*He would destroy the temple.*" No, Jesus said he would raise it up, and he wasn't speaking of a literal temple (John 2:19; Mark 14:58). There is no need for a Third Temple to be rebuilt. How would that glorify God? In light of Paul's epistles, *we* are His temple.

> I did not see a temple in the city, because *the Lord God Almighty and the Lamb are its temple.* The city does not need the sun or the moon to shine on it, for the glory of God gives it light, and the Lamb is its lamp.
> —Revelation 21:22–23

There is no need for a temple in Heavenly Jerusalem. Unlike His fear-inducing Presence at Mt. Sinai in the form of a thick cloud accompanied by thunder, lightning, and a loud voice, in the New Jerusalem, God will display his glory in splendor and light. We get glimpses of His glory occasionally in the present; we await the full revelation of His glory at the Second Coming.

> You have not come to a mountain that can be touched and that is burning with fire; to darkness, gloom and storm ... But *you have come to Mount Zion, to the city of the living God, the heavenly Jerusalem.*
> —Hebrews 12:18, 22

We can only dream what our future will be like when Christ returns. Will we join our departed loved ones in spirit form in Paradise while we await God's restoration of the old heavens and earth that are to be destroyed by fire on the day of judgment (2 Peter 3:7, 10)? Will we receive our glorified body when we enter into the new heavens and earth? This is where a parable from Jesus would be helpful. He was a master at communicating the intended simplicity, made so confusing by the footnotes of man. In the meantime, we can pray to "him who is able to do immeasurably more than all we ask or imagine" (Ephesians 3:20). Apparently, our minds are incapable of even conceiving the things God has in store for those who put their faith in Him. If you are anything like me, you can imagine some pretty amazing things.

It would be wonderful to be alive when Christ returns, to meet and join the saints who are with him in the heavens before the Final Judgment, but I suspect that I will be among those who have "fallen asleep in the Lord." The good news is, the dead in Christ shall be the first to meet him in the air.[80] There they will welcome the living who are to be caught up to join them, accompanying him to heaven while the new heavens and new earth are being prepared. How long that will take, only God knows.

> They came to life and reigned with Christ for a thousand years. (The rest of the dead did not come to life until the thousand years were ended.) This is the first resurrection. Blessed and holy are those who share in the first resurrection. The second death has no power over them, but they will be priests of God and of Christ and will reign with him for a thousand years.
> —Revelation 20:4–6

---

[80] 1 Thessalonians 4:13–18. These verses describe the events of the rapture of the living saints.

CHAPTER 12:

Prophecy Is Not "Rocket Science"

Having begun in grace, let us not return to the old ways of the Mosaic law, as Scofield would have us do. Is today's Church going to reject Jesus all over again? "God forbid!" Paul would say. But how do we avoid making the same mistake that Israel did in the first century? Do we really want Jesus to return in power, like all the other empires of the past? The Jewish community discovered in the most horrific of fashions during the Holocaust of the 1940s how power in the hands of a few can be grossly abused. Zechariah 4:6 states, *"Not by might, nor by power,* but by My Spirit says the LORD." Yet, incredibly, Scofield says in his footnote on Zechariah 12:8, "The kingdom is to be established *by power,* not persuasion, and is to follow divine judgment upon the Gentile world powers."[81] How do we square that with Jesus' own words in the book of Mark?

> After John was put in prison, Jesus went into Galilee, proclaiming the good news of God. *The time is fulfilled,* he said. *The kingdom of God is at hand*; Repent and believe the good news!
> —Mark 1:14–15

> Truly I tell you, some who are standing here will not taste death before they see that *the kingdom of God has come with power.*
> —Mark 9:1

---

[81] *New Scofield Reference Bible,* (1967), p. 974, note 1, III, 2, e (italics added).

Two things should immediately jump out: (1) the kingdom of God *has come*; it is not awaiting fulfillment in the future; and (2) some of the people then living would bear witness, by means of power, that God's kingdom had come. Jesus wanted no part of the kind of earthly power that is granted by becoming a king. If Jesus were to come with military might, then how would he be different from a Napoleon or a Hitler? When the people wanted to make him king by force, we are told that he withdrew to a mountain by himself, presumably to pray (John 6:15). Does this sound like the Warrior-King Messiah that the Jews in the first century, and Scofield's followers today, were looking for? No! Jesus is offering a different form of exodus—a deliverance from spiritual exile. His kingdom is spiritual in nature, spread by persuasion and the preaching of the Gospel, not at the end of a gun or tank!

The "KISS" Principle

Eschatology is not the "rocket science" that End-Times "gurus" would have you believe. There is a reason Jesus taught in parables. Today we call it the KISS principle—"Keep It Simple Stupid." He wanted his listeners to understand what he was talking about. It is true that he occasionally used cryptic language when Roman spies were lurking about or to point out the Pharisees' hardness of heart. There was precedent for this:

> He said, Go and tell this people: Be ever hearing, but never understanding; be ever seeing, but never perceiving. Make the heart of this people calloused; make their ears dull and close their eyes. Otherwise they might see with their eyes, hear with their ears, understand with their hearts, and turn and be healed.
> –Isaiah 6:9–10

All four Gospel writers record this passage from Isaiah 6:9–10 as part of Jesus' reply to the disciples' inquiry, "Why do you speak to the people in parables?" (Matthew 13:13; Mark 4:12; Luke 8; John 12:40). Jesus turns to two passages in Isaiah in his response—the one quoted above and Isaiah 53:1, "Lord, who has believed our message and to whom has the arm of the Lord been revealed?" It is no coincidence that Jesus pointed to Isaiah's description of the "Suffering Servant." Christians look back upon history and see Isaiah 53 fulfilled by Christ's sacrifice of himself, right along with the other lambs, at Passover (1 Corinthians 5:7–8):

> He was despised and rejected by mankind, a man of suffering, and familiar with pain ... Surely he took up our pain and bore our suffering ... He was pierced for our transgressions, he was crushed for our iniquities... and by his wounds we are healed ... the Lord has laid on him the iniquity of us all. He was oppressed and afflicted, yet he did not open his mouth... he was led like a lamb to the slaughter, and as a sheep before its shearers is silent, so he did not open his mouth. He was *cut off* from the land of the living.
>
> –Isaiah 53:3–8

The narrative in John 12 reveals more of the details:

> Even after Jesus had performed so many signs in their presence, *they still would not believe in him. This was to fulfill the word of Isaiah* the prophet: Lord, who has believed our message and to whom has the arm of the Lord been revealed? For this reason they could not believe, because, as Isaiah says elsewhere: He has blinded their eyes and hardened their hearts, so they can neither see with their eyes, nor understand with their hearts, nor turn— and I would heal them. *Isaiah said this because he saw Jesus' glory and spoke about him.*
>
> –John 12:37ff

Isaiah, like Abraham, saw Jesus' day and looked forward to his glorious coming. John's Gospel combines two of Isaiah's prophecies. First, that of Jesus as the fulfillment of God's Servant, who was to suffer on our behalf, taking upon himself the punishment for our sins. Second, Israel's stubborn refusal to believe in God's Anointed, resulting in a diagnosis of "hardness of the heart" and "blindness of eye." People lament when pastors compromise their sermons for fear of offending someone in their congregations. We shouldn't be too quick to point the finger, however, for we are all guilty of this in some aspect or another. This is not a modern phenomenon, for the admonition, "Whoever is ashamed of me and my words, the Son of Man will be ashamed of them when he comes in his glory…" applies to us all (Mark 8:38; Luke 9:26).

Some things are none of our business, and personally, I believe God intentionally left some things obscure in order to force us to study and pray to seek His guidance. God *could* have made it easy for us. He could have said, "I am coming back in the year _____."

There must be a good reason for Him not to do so.

In the meantime, we should be about the Great Commission. 'All authority has been given to me in heaven, and on earth. Therefore, go and make disciples of all nations, baptizing them in the name of the Father and of the Son and of the Holy Spirit" (Matthew 28:18–19). We know we are on safe ground if our message to the world is, "Jesus is Lord!" That was the message in the days of the Caesars; it is just as important today. Contrary to current popular belief, Putin will soon stand in the Judgment just as all the tyrants before him. In this current era where it is difficult to decipher falsehood from truth, as political factions wrangle to maintain power, it is all the more critical for Believers to cling to the bedrock of absolute truth found in the Lord Jesus Christ.

CONCLUSION

Are we living in the final generation of human history? Is the Second Coming of Christ imminent? We can't say for sure; not even Jesus knows the day. He will come when his heavenly Father tells him it is time. It is easy to understand why many people fear they are living in the last days. The populations of the world today resemble those in the days of the tower of Babel when the Lord said, "If as one people speaking the same language they have begun to do this, then nothing they plan to do will be impossible for them" (Genesis 11:6). English is now spoken in most countries, and even more significantly, the language of computers, 1 and 0, have united scientists across the globe, emboldening them to pursue dreams of creating life on their own. If God intervened at Babel by confounding and scattering the people, it is not difficult to imagine Him stepping in again to prevent mankind from playing "god."

End-times fiction novels have prepped millions of Christians to see the "mark of the beast" behind every new technological advancement.[82] We are now witnessing the proliferation of nuclear weapons in countries that appear eager to use them. The recent pandemic has emboldened some government officials to abuse their positions of power, as they indefinitely extend rules that were intended for short-term emergency use only. Political "science" is running rough-shod over common sense. Our laws are repeatedly ignored, allowing acts of violence to escalate at an alarming rate in

---

[82] Scanning machines at supermarkets raised many Christians eyebrows when they were first utilized. Recently, thousands have refused the Covid-19 vaccine for fear that it might contain nanobots, which they associate with the mark of the beast.

urban centers. Corporations are being pressured to force the administration of medical procedures on their employees despite opposition by a significant percentage of the population. The *recommendations* of health care providers are pushed aside to make room for the politically-motivated enforcement of *mandates*—something we associate with Third-World Banana Republics, not America. Media pundits offer such disparate opinions on world events that people are left asking, "Who/what do we believe anymore?" Probably how the disciples felt once their leader, their Lord, was crucified. They immediately scattered, and it only took days before they scampered back to their old ways of life. I love the way the Gospel of John ends, for it leaves us with great hope for the future.

In John 21, a man stands on the shore as seven former disciples of Jesus are fishing and says, "Friends, haven't you any fish?" They do not realize it is Jesus. "No," they answered. The man directs them to throw their net on the right side of the boat, even though they have been out there all night with no luck. When they did, they caught so many fish they were unable to haul the catch into the boat. John, the beloved disciple of Jesus, is first to recognize the master, saying to Peter, "It is the Lord!" Peter is the first to get to shore. There he is greeted by a charcoal fire. His heart must have broken, as it was just days before that he had warmed himself by a charcoal fire as he denied knowing Jesus.[83] Peter's heart must have broken a second time when Jesus asked him for the third time, "Do you love me?" But the third time, Jesus used a lesser word for love, in essence—"Peter, do you even like me?"[84] Jesus' intent is never to

---

[83] N.T. Wright, *John For Everyone,* Part 2, Chapters 11-21, (Louisville: Westminster John Knox Press, 2004), 158-159. Attention is drawn to the fact that these were charcoal fires; there seems to have been a reason for this.

[84] The first two times Jesus uses the strong word *agape* for love. The third time he uses the lesser word *phileō*. *Phileō* also means "love" (brotherly love), but I used *"like"* here as a means of conveying how it probably felt to Peter.

Conclusion

crush anyone, however, and he gently restores his former disciple by thrusting him back into service with the three-fold command, "Feed my sheep." There are times when the LORD can only get our full attention by means of pain and suffering. More than once Scripture reminds us, "The LORD chastens the ones He loves."[85] Notice the angel's words to the women at the empty tomb, "Go, tell his disciples, *and Peter*." Peter may not have considered himself a disciple when he first came on shore, but he did after spending a few moments with Jesus.

Salvation is the primary theme in this story, just as it was in the kingdom parables, and not merely the salvation of Peter. When Jesus says to Peter, "Bring some of the fish you have just caught," we are told that the number of fish caught was 153. Why 153? Many creative calculations and suggestions have been made, but I suggest that the answer is right before our eyes, and it all points once again to salvation. Noah and his family survived the Flood by spending time with a cargo of smelly animals in a wooden "fish" for … *150 days*.[86] Jonah spent time sloshing around the smelly belly of a literal fish for … *3 days*.[87] Jesus now stands on the shore like a fish out of water using 153 fish to demonstrate that salvation is available to the entire world.† But time may be running out.

Revelation 20:2–3 tells us that Satan was to be bound for 1,000 years, after which he would be let loose for a short season. Have the 1,000 years come to an end? We don't know. What we do know, according to Jesus, is that Satan, the "strong man," was in the process of being bound as his kingdom continued to expand.[88] When was Satan "locked up"? At the cross; more specifically, at Christ's resurrection. But what about the "1,000 years"? For some it

---

[85] Proverbs 3:11–12; Psalm 94:12; Job 5:17; Hebrews 12:6; 1 Corinthians 11:32; Revelation 3:19.
[86] Genesis 7:24; 8:3.
[87] Jonah 1:17.
[88] Matthew 12:28–29; quoting Isaiah 49:25.

represents a golden era when Jesus will rule over the nations with a "rod of iron" from his throne in Jerusalem (Premillennialists). Others anticipate a continued expansion of world-wide Christian dominion when a majority of people will believe in Christ when he returns (Postmillennialists). Still others do not expect any kind of literal fulfillment in regards to the "1,000 years" (Amillennialists). For them, the "1,000 years" is a symbolic number. It merely represents the span of time between the "binding" of Satan and his being "set free" once those years have come to a close.

The Premillennialists and Amillennialists are both pessimistic about the future advances of the Church. Postmillennialists are optimistic, but many consider them to be too optimistic (especially after World Wars I and II). What if none of them are correct? Perhaps it is as simple as Christians being obedient to the Great Commission during this time of Satan being bound, praying for endurance when he is "let loose" to gather all the enemies of the Church together for one, last gasp effort to thwart the promises of God (Satan, in his arrogance, will likely be allowed to think that he has escaped from his "prison," emboldening him even further). But rather than living in a constant state of fear of the State, wondering what liberties will be taken away next, Christians need to remind themselves, "Jesus is Lord." Our freedom lies in resting in the Lord Jesus Christ. In the meantime, it is imperative that we:

> Go therefore and make disciples of all nations, baptizing them in the name of the Father and of the Son and of the Holy Spirit, and teaching them to obey everything I have commanded you. And surely I am with you always, to the very end of the age.
>
> –Matthew 28:19–20

My prayer is that you will get a study Bible with large margins and fill in those margins with your own notes, questions, cross references, and illustrations and launch into a lifetime journey

Conclusion

of discovery of our God's wonderful Word. In your times of study, never forget the wisdom (and humor) in the ancient Chinese proverb—"It is very difficult to prophesy, especially about the future."

I leave you with one of my favorite quotes, from 13th Century Suffi poet Jelaluddin Rumi—

> Beyond right thinking and wrong thinking, there is a field;
> I will meet you there.

APPENDIX A

FULFILLMENT OF DANIEL 9:24'S CHECKLIST OF EVENTS

1. To finish the transgression

When Jesus picked up the cup at the Last Supper and stated, "This cup is the *new covenant in my blood*, which is poured out for you," he was proclaiming the finish of the transgression of sin. He was ushering in the covenant that the Jews should have recognized from the prophet Jeremiah,

> The days are coming, declares the Lord, when *I will make a new covenant* with the people of Israel and with the people of Judah. It will not be like the covenant I made with their ancestors ... which they broke ... For I will forgive their wickedness and will remember their sins no more.
> —Jeremiah 31:31–34

Covenant and testament are the same Greek word, *diathēkē* (διαθηκη). In confirming this new covenant with his own blood, Jesus gave us the name *New Testament*. The author of the book of Hebrews confirms this:

> And for this cause he [Jesus] is the mediator of the new covenant/testament that by means of death, *for the redemption of the transgressions* that were under the first covenant, they which are called might receive the promise of eternal inheritance.
> —Hebrews 9:15

Appendix

This should come as no surprise. Why else would the prophet Isaiah tell us the Servant of the LORD would be *pierced and crushed*? We are not left to guess. He tells us, "He was pierced *for our transgressions*, he was crushed *for our iniquities*" (Isaiah 53:5).

2. To make an end of sin

Do you remember why the angel told Joseph and Mary to name their child "Jesus"? The opening chapter of the Gospel tells us, "Give him the name 'Jesus,' for he will *save the people from their sins*" (Matthew 1:21). Once again, Hebrews testifies to this act of Jesus:

> Otherwise Christ would have had to suffer many times since the creation of the world. But he has appeared once for all at the culmination of the ages *to do away with sin* by the sacrifice of himself.
> –Hebrews 9:26

> The Holy Spirit also testifies to us about this. First, he says: This is the covenant I will make with them after that time, says the Lord. I will put my laws in their hearts, and I will write them in their minds. Then he adds, *Their sins and lawless acts I will remember no more*.
> –Hebrews 10:15–17

3. To atone for wickedness

How is wickedness/sin atoned for? In Israel of the Old Testament, it was by means of a once yearly animal sacrifice at the Feast of Atonement. It was more of an I. O. U., as it did not pay for sin but merely covered it over for another year (atonement is *kippur,* which means "to cover"). The people of Israel did not see this act, as it occurred within the Holy of Holies of the temple, but they did see the pre-enactment of this sacrifice by means of the "escape goat." This is when the high priest laid his hands on the escape goat, polluting the goat with the nation's sins prior to symbolically removing their sins as far as the east is from the west by releasing the goat into the wilderness. Isaiah spoke of the Suffering Servant's role in Atonement when he states,

> But he was pierced for our transgressions, he was crushed for our iniquities; the punishment that brought us peace was on him, and by his wounds we are healed. We all, like sheep, have gone astray, each of us has turned to our own way; and the LORD has *laid on him the iniquity* of us all.
> –Isaiah 53:5–6

"Laid" here is reminiscent of the high priest laying his hands on the escape goat in Leviticus 16:8-10,20-22. Messiah, as the Suffering Servant, would take upon himself the sins of the world. Jesus fulfilled both roles of the Feast of Atonement. First, he bore the sins of the people with his own blood into the real Holy of Holies, once for all, before sitting at the right hand of the Father (Hebrews 10:10–12). Second, since no one got to see this happen, the glorified Jesus appeared to his disciples and said, "Peace be with you!" Then he said to Thomas, "Put your finger here; see my hands. Reach out your hand and put it into my side. Stop doubting and believe" (John 20:19–29).[89] Here are three other verses attesting to the fact that Jesus atoned for wickedness:

> Hebrews 2:17—that he might make *atonement for the sins* of the people
> 2 Corinthians 5:19—God was reconciling ... not counting people's sins against them
> Titus 2:14—who gave himself for us *to redeem us from all wickedness*

---

[89] Thomas was not there the week before, when Jesus first appeared to the disciples, and could not bring himself to believe them. He famously declared, 'Unless I see the nail marks in his hands and put my finger where the nails were, and put my hand into his side, I will not believe."

Appendix

4. To bring in everlasting righteousness

Two Old Testament prophets, Isaiah and Jeremiah, spoke of the "Branch" that the LORD would raise up for David, who would execute justice and righteousness. Both prophets ascribe unique features of this "Branch, because the Spirit of the LORD will rest upon him." In fact, *"The LORD our righteousness"* (*Yahweh tsidkenu*) is one of the seven covenant names of God.[90]

> A shoot will come up from the stump of Jesse; from his roots, a *Branch* will bear fruit. The Spirit of the Lord will rest on him ... He will not judge by what he sees with his eyes, or decide by what he hears with his ears; but with *righteousness* he will judge.
> —Isaiah 11:1–4

> The days are coming, declares the Lord, when I will raise up for David a Righteous *Branch* ... This is the name by which he will be called: The Lord Our *Righteousness*.
> —Jeremiah 23:5–6

Jesus was from the royal lineage of David; and it was Jesus, not Solomon, who would establish David's house and kingdom that would endure forever (2 Samuel 7:16). Several New Testament passages point to Jesus as the fulfillment of this "righteous Branch." In Revelation 19:11, Jesus is the One riding upon a white horse:

> And I saw heaven opened, and behold, a white horse, and He who sat on it is called Faithful and True, and *in righteousness He judges* and wages war.

---

[90] The seven covenant names of God are: *Yahweh jireh* ("The LORD appears/provides," Genesis 22:13); *Yahweh rapha* ("The LORD our healer," Exodus 15:26); *Yahweh nissi* ("The LORD our banner," Exodus 17:15); *Yahweh shalom* ("The LORD our peace," Judges 6:24); *Yahweh rohi* ("The LORD our shepherd," Psalm 23:1); *Yahweh tsidkenu* ("The LORD our righteousness," Jeremiah 23:6); and *Yahweh shammah* ("The LORD is there," Ezekiel 48:35).

The righteousness that Jesus brings is an everlasting righteousness—

> So that, just as sin reigned in death, so also grace might reign *through righteousness to bring eternal life* through Jesus Christ our Lord.
> —Romans 5:21

When did Jesus receive the authority to usher in everlasting righteousness? At his baptism—

> Then Jesus came from Galilee to the Jordan to be baptized by John. But John tried to deter him, saying, I need to be baptized by you, and do you come to me? Jesus replied, Let it be so now; *it is proper for us to do this to fulfill all righteousness.* Then John consented.
> —Matthew 3:13–15

It was by means of his suffering that Jesus provides us with the ability to live for righteousness. 1 Peter 2:24 states, "He himself bore our sins in his body on the cross, *so that we might die to sins and live for righteousness*; by his wounds you have been healed."

5. To seal up vision and prophecy

In Matthew 11, the imprisoned John the Baptist sent his disciples to Jesus to inquire whether or not he really was the Messiah. After pointing out all the miraculous deeds that were being performed—the blind receive sight, the lame walk, those who have leprosy are cleansed, the deaf hear, the dead are raised, and the good news is proclaimed to the poor—Jesus said to the crowd, "For all the Prophets and the Law prophesied *until John.* And if you are willing to accept it, he is the Elijah who was to come" (see Matthew 11:13–14; 17:10–12). "This is the one about whom it is written: 'I will send my messenger ahead of you, who will prepare your way before you.'" John the Baptist was the last of the Old Testament prophets, fulfilling the role of "Elijah" in Malachi 4:5, "See, I will send the prophet Elijah to you before that great and dreadful day of the Lord comes." There is no need for vision and prophecy once the Messiah is here, it has been "sealed up."

6. To anoint the most holy

"Anoint" is from the Hebrew word *mashiach*, from which the title Messiah is drawn. Some translations interpret Daniel 9:24 as "to anoint the most holy [place]." While at times inanimate objects such as an altar were anointed, typically it referred to the pouring of oil upon a prophet, priest, or king to confer authority upon an individual to coincide with their title. The Old Testament speaks of a coming Deliverer who would bear the title of Messiah—"Anointed One" (Psalm 2:2; Daniel 9:25–26). The physical enactment of anointing was the representation of the *spiritual* effects placed on the one receiving the Holy Spirit. Jesus was anointed at his baptism:

> Then John gave this testimony: I saw the Spirit come down from heaven as a dove and remain on him. And I myself did not know him, but the one who sent me to baptize with water told me, The man on whom you see *the Spirit come down and remain* is the one who will baptize with the Holy Spirit. I have seen and I testify that this is God's Chosen One.
> –John 1:32–34

The word "anointed" does not appear in the baptism narrative in John, but Acts 10:37–38 makes this connection:

> You know what has happened throughout the province of Judea, beginning in Galilee after the baptism that John preached—how *God anointed Jesus of Nazareth with the Holy Spirit and power.*

Further proof of his anointing is found in the account of Jesus reading from the scroll of Isaiah in the synagogue of Nazareth. Jesus read these words from Isaiah 61:1–2,

> The Spirit of the Sovereign Lord is on me, because *the Lord has anointed me* to proclaim good news to the poor... He has sent me to bind up the brokenhearted, to proclaim freedom for the captives and release from darkness for the prisoners, to proclaim the year of the Lord's favor.

After returning the scroll, he sat down and said, "*Today this scripture is fulfilled in your hearing.*" He is emphatically declaring that the LORD has poured His Spirit on him, has *anointed* him to perform the very things that were reported back to John the Baptist as the signs that he indeed was the coming "Anointed One," the Messiah. Significantly, he did not finish Isaiah's sentence in 61:2, "... and the day of vengeance of our God." That would not happen for another generation. As it was, his hometown citizens tried to kill him (Luke 4:14–30).

So, in answer to the question, "Did Jesus Christ fulfill all of these six things articulated in Daniel 9:24?" the answer is a resounding, "Yes!"

APPENDIX B

PROOF THAT BARNEY THE DINOSAUR IS THE ANTICHRIST

Given: Barney is a cute purple dinosaur.

Prove: Barney is the Antichrist (666).

CUTE PURPLE DINOSAUR; change U's to V's, which is proper in Latin.

CVTE PVRPLE DINOSAVR; extract out all of the Roman numerals.

CVVLDIV; convert the Roman numerals into their Arabic values.

$$C \quad V \quad V \quad L \quad D \quad I \quad V$$

$$100+ \quad 5+ \quad 5+ \quad 50+ \quad 500+ \quad 1+ \quad 5 \quad =666$$

There you have it—proof that Barney the dinosaur is the Antichrist.[91]

---

[91] Robert G. Clouse, Robert Hosack, Richard V Pierard, *The New Millennium Manual: A Once and Future Guide*, (Eugene, OR: Wipf and Stock Publishers, 1999), 171.

If you liked the book,
be sure to leave a review
and share it with your friends
on social media.

For more information, go to:
donh.authorchannel.com

Appendix

BIBLIOGRAPHY

Arnt, William F. and F. Wilbur Gingrich. *Greek-English Lexicon of the New Testament and Other Early Christian Literature.* Chicago: The University of Chicago Press, 1958.

Bahnsen, Greg. *Defending the Christian Worldview Against All Opposition, Series One: Weapons of Our Spiritual Warfare.* Powder Springs, GA: American Vision, 2006.

Boettner, Loraine. *The Millennium.* Phillipsburg, NJ: Presbyterian and Reformed Publishing Company, 1957.

Brown, Francis, S.R. Driver, and Charles A. Briggs. *The Brown-Driver-Briggs Hebrew and English Lexicon.* Peabody, MA: Hendrickson Publishers, 2005.

Cahn, Jonathan. *The Paradigm: The Ancient Blueprint That Holds the Mystery of Our Times.* Lake Mary, FL: FrontLine Charisma Media/Charisma House Book Group, 1917.

Caird, G. B. *Black's New Testament Commentary: The Revelation of Saint John.* Peabody, MA: Hendrickson Publishers, 1966.

Canfield, Joseph M. *The Incredible Scofield and His Book.* Vallecito, CA: Ross House Books, 1988.

Caringola, Robert. *Seventy Weeks: The Historical Alternative.* Shippensburg, PA: 1991.

Carrington, Philip. *The Meaning of the Revelation.* Eugene, OR: Wipf and Stock Publishers, *1931.*

Champlin, Edward. *Nero.* London: The Belknap Press of Harvard University Press, 2003.

Chilton, David. *Paradise Restored: A Biblical Theology of Dominion*. Ft. Worth, TX: Dominion Press, 1985.

Chilton, David. *The Days of Vengeance: An Exposition of the Book of Revelation*. Ft. Worth, TX: Dominion Press, 1987.

Chilton, David. *The Great Tribulation*. Fort Worth, TX: Dominion Press, 1987.

Clouse, Robert G., Robert Hosack, and Richard V. Pierard. *The New Millennium Manual: A Once and Future Guide*. Eugene, OR: Wipf and Stock Publishers, 1999.

DeMar, Gary. *Is Jesus Coming Soon?* Powder Springs, GA: American Vision, Inc., 2006.

DeMar, Gary. *The Gog and Magog End-Time Alliance: Israel, Russia, and Syria in Bible Prophecy,* Powder Springs, GA: American Vision Press, 2016.

Gentry, Kenneth L. *Before Jerusalem Fell: Dating the Book of Revelation, An Exegetical and Historical Argument for a Pre-A.D. 70 Composition*. Tyler, TX: Institute for Christian Economics, 1989.

Grant, Michael. *The Twelve Caesars*. New York: Barnes & Noble Books, 1996.

Hendriksen, William. *More Than Conquerors: An Interpretation of the Book of Revelation*. Grand Rapids: Baker Book House, 1940.

Howard, Kevin and Marvin Rosenthal. *The Feasts of the LORD: God's Prophetic Calendar From Calvary to the Kingdom*. Nashville: Thomas Nelson, Inc., Publishers, 1997.

Irenaeus. *Against Heresies*.

Johnson, Dennis E. *Triumph of the Lamb: A Commentary on Revelation*. Phillipsburg, NJ: Presbyterian and Reformed Publishing Company, 2001.

Jordan, James B. *Esther in the Midst of Covenant History*. Niceville, FL: Biblical Horizons, 1995.

Josephus, Flavius. *Works*. Translated by William Whiston. Four vols. Grand Rapids: Baker Book House, 1974.

Kik, Marcellus. *An Eschatology of Victory*. Phillipsburg, NJ: Presbyterian and Reformed Publishing Company, 1971.

Kline, Meredith G. *God, Heaven and Har Magedon: A Covenantal Tale of Cosmos and Telos*. Eugene, OR: Wipf and Stock Publishers, 2006.

Kline, Meredith G. *Kingdom Prologue: Genesis Foundations for a Covenantal Worldview*. Overland Park, KS: Two Age Press, 2000

Larkin, Clarence. *Dispensational Truth or God's Plan and Purpose in the Ages*. Glenside, PA: Rev. Clarence Larkin Est., 1918.

Lightner, Robert P. *The Last Days Handbook: A Comprehensive Guide to Understanding the Different Views of Prophecy*. Nashville: Thomas Nelson Publishers, 1990.

Lindsey, Hal. *The Late Great Planet Earth*. Grand Rapids: Zondervan, 1970.

Lindsey, Hal. *The 1980s: Countdown to Armageddon*. San Francisco: Westgate Press, 1980.

MacPherson, Dave. *The Rapture Plot*. Muskogee, OK: Artisan Publishers, 1994.

Masselink, Rev. William. *Why Thousand Years? or Will The Second Coming Be Pre-Millennial?* Grand Rapids: Wm. B. Eerdmans Publishing Company, 1953.

Mauro, Philip. *The Patmos Visions: A Study of the Apocalypse.* Boston: Hamilton Bros., 1925.

Mauro, Philip. *The Seventy Weeks and the Great Tribulation: A Study of the Last Two Visions of Daniel, and of the Olivet Discourse of the Lord Jesus Christ.* Middletown, DE: Ravensbrook Publishers, 1921, reprinted 2014.

Metzger, Bruce M. *A Textual Commentary on the Greek New Testament.* Stuttgart: German Bible Society, 1994.

Mounce, Robert H. *The New International Commentary on the New Testament: The Book of Revelation.* Grand Rapids: William B. Eerdmans Publishing Company, 1977.

Owen, Paul. *The Origin of Futurism and Preterism.* Owasso, OK: Truth in History Ministries, 2006.

Popper, K.R. *The Open Society and Its Enemies*, Volume II, The high tide of prophecy: Hegel, Marx and the Aftermath, London: Routledge and Kegan Paul, 1945, 5th ed., 1966.

Riddlebarger, Kim. *The Man of Sin: Uncovering the Truth About the Antichrist.* Grand Rapids, MI: Baker Books, 2006.

Rogers, Jay. *In The Days Of These Kings: The Book of Daniel in Preterist Perspective.* Clermont, FL: Media House International, 2017.

Roth, Cecil. *Encyclopedia Judaica:* Volume 6. Jerusalem: Keter Publishing House Jerusalem Ltd., 1972.

Rushdoony, Rousas John. *Thy Kingdom Come: Studies in Daniel and Revelation.* Vallecito, CA: Ross House Books, 2001.

Appendix

Russell, J. Stuart. *The Parousia: A Study of the New Testament Doctrine of Our Lord's Second Coming.* Grand Rapids: Baker Book House, 1985.

Schweitzer, Albert. *The Quest of the Historical Jesus: A Critical Study of Its Progress from Reimarus to Wrede.* New York: The Macmillan Company, 1961.

Seekins, Dr. Frank T. *Hebrew Word Pictures: How Does The Hebrew Alphabet Reveal Prophetic Truths.* Phoenix: Living Word Pictures Inc., 2003.

Talbert, Charles H. *The Apocalypse: A Reading of the Revelation of John.* Louisville, KY: Westminster John Knox Press, 1994.

Terry, Milton. *Biblical Apocalyptics: A Study of the Most Notable Revelations of God and of Christ in the Canonical Scriptures.* Eugene, OR: Wipf and Stock Publishers, 2001, previously published by Eaton & Mains, NY, 1898.

Terry, Milton. *Biblical Hermeneutics, Second Edition: A Treatise on the Interpretation of the Old and New Testaments.* Grand Rapids: Zondervan Publishing House, 1974, previously published by Hunt and Eason, 1890, Evanston, IL.

Willis, Mike. *A Study of the A.D. 70 Doctrine Realized Eschatology: A Compendium of Articles for Study.* Athens, AL: Truth Publications, Inc., 2018.

Wohlberg, Steve. *End Time Delusions: The Rapture, the Antichrist, Israel, and the End of the World.* Shippensburg, PA: Destiny Image Publishers, 2004.

Woodrow, Ralph. *Great Prophecies of the Bible.* Riverside, CA: Ralph Woodrow Evangelical Association, Inc., 1989.

Woodrow, Ralph. *His Truth Is Marching On: Advanced Studies on Prophecy in the Light of History.* Riverside, CA: Ralph Woodrow Evangelistic Association, Inc., 1977.

Wright, N. T. *Jesus and the Victory of God*. Minneapolis: Fortress Press, 1996.

Wright, N. T. *John For Everyone,* Part 2. Louisville: Westminster John Knox Press, 2004.

Wright, N. T. *The New Testament and the People of God*. Minneapolis: Fortress Press, 1992.

Young, Edward J. *Daniel.* Grand Rapids: Eerdmans Publishing Company, 1949.

ABOUT THE AUTHOR

Dr. Donald Hobson is a retired dentist who practiced in Birch Run, MI for 33 years. Dr. Hobson began his collegiate education at Taylor University and holds degrees from Michigan State (B.S.), the University of Michigan (DDS), and Biola (Masters Degree in Christian Apologetics). He studied Hebrew and Greek at Western Theological Seminary.

Dr. Hobson spent the last thirty years whitening and straightening people's teeth; now he hopes to spend the next twenty or thirty years, Lord willing, straightening out what he perceives to be "crooked thinking." The study of theology has always been more than a hobby for Dr. Hobson, as he has taught youth groups or adults nearly every weekend for the past forty years. His passion is to see his students develop a similar love for the Scripture and to think for themselves.

The driving force for pursuing theological studies stemmed from his desire to understand the Book of Revelation. That pursuit still continues, as the interpretations tendered for that fascinating and mysterious book range from the ridiculous to the incomprehensible. He is currently working on several books, this being his first published work.

He and his wife, Tracie, have been married for nearly forty years, have raised five children, numerous dogs and cats, and are the proud grandparents of three boys (with another grandchild on the way). They currently reside in Flushing, MI, their homestead for the last thirty-one years.

Made in the USA
Monee, IL
28 October 2022

77f7ea75-759f-49d4-8dc9-c2ad491f6283R01